In Covenant with God

Builders of Hope
    Book 1
        In Covenant with God
    Book 2
        Followers of Jesus
    Book 3
        Acting Through History
    Book 4
        Committed as Church
    Book 5
        Fostering Culture and Society

Forjadores de Esperanza
    Libro 1
        En Alianza con Dios
    Libro 2
        Seguidores de Jesús
    Libro 3
        Activos en la Historia
    Libro 4
        Comprometidos como Iglesia
    Libro 5
        Constructores de Cultura y Sociedad

🝊 Builders of Hope 🝊

Book 1

In Covenant with God

In Covenant with God Editorial Team

Saint Mary's Press
Christian Brothers Publications
Winona, Minnesota

OF HOPE

WITNESSES

Genuine recycled paper with 10% post-consumer waste.
Printed with soy-based ink.

The publishing team for this volume included Eduardo Arnouil, development editor; Jacqueline M. Captain, manuscript editor; Amy Schlumpf Manion, typesetter; Maurine R. Twait, art director; Alicia María Sánchez, cover designer and illustrator; Kent Linder, graphic designer; pre-press, printing, and binding by the graphics division of Saint Mary's Press.

Saint Mary's Press wishes to give special acknowledgment to the ACTA Foundation, for funding that helped to subsidize this publication.

The acknowledgments continue on page 198.

Printed in the United States of America

Printing: 9 8 7 6 5 4 3 2 1

Year: 2006 05 04 03 02 01 00 99 98

ISBN 0-88489-437-1

In Covenant with God Editorial Team

General Editor:	Carmen María Cervantes, EdD
Writers:	Eduardo Arnouil
	Carlos Carrillo
	Pedro Castex
	Carmen María Cervantes, EdD
	Juan Díaz-Vilar, SJ
	Rev. Juan J. Huitrado-Rizo
	Edmundo Rodríguez, SJ
Consultants:	Alejandro Aguilera-Titus
	Rev. Juan Alfaro, PhD
	Dolores Díez-de-Sollano, SH
	Antonio Medina-Rivera, PhD
	Leticia Medina
Translator into English:	Richard Wood, PhD
Secretaries:	Aurora Macías-Dewhirst
	José María Matty-Cervantes

CONTENTS

In Covenant with God is the first book in the Builders of Hope series. This series was written to promote the development of lay vocation among *jóvenes** in the church and in society. *In Covenant with God* is intended for participants sixteen years of age and older who are in small missionary and evangelizing communities. If used with younger adolescents, it will require adaptations in methodology and substance. It is also suitable for groups of *jóvenes* and for other pastoral settings.

In Covenant with God is designed to begin a process of continuous evangelization and integral formation that leads to a **Christian praxis** once the participants have had a basic experience of life in a community. Its objectives are to lead the participants to discover themselves as persons, to help them understand the meaning of the Covenant with God, and to promote their living out the Covenant both personally and communally. The book emphasizes the vocation and mission of *jóvenes* in salvation history from a **theological** and an **anthropological** perspective.

This book follows the Prophets of Hope model, which is described in the books *The Prophets of Hope Model: A Weekend Workshop* and *Dawn on the Horizon: Creating Small Communities*. For the location of *In Covenant with God* as a resource for the implementation of the model, see appendix 2.

The process of *In Covenant with God* consists of *an initial journey* that helps the participants understand the meaning of the Covenant; *two cycles of community meetings* that focus on various aspects of the Covenant, from the perspective of both the Old and New Testaments; *a formation workshop* that offers an introduction to the study of the Bible; and *a retreat* that is designed to motivate the

---

*The first time any special term appears, it is presented in boldfaced type. Definitions can be found in the glossary. We suggest that before reading the book, you review the glossary to acquaint yourself with this vocabulary. We also recommend that persons responsible for coordinating and facilitating the meetings carefully study any special terminology used.

participants to live the Covenant at the personal and communal levels. In addition, the book contains *three documents* and *two appendices*. The documents offer different kinds of information necessary for the comprehension of and reflection on the themes that integrate the formation process. The appendices include evaluation forms and a chart of the Witnesses of Hope collection.

This book is an instrument to support the life of a community. Each community should use this resource to the extent that it helps to develop the community's Christian life and strengthen its missionary spirit. It is recommended that the participants keep a diary with their reflections or, at least, take notes in their books.

Methodology of the Builders of Hope series

The Builders of Hope series follows a methodology based on a holistic perspective of young people's human development and Christian growth. It promotes critical analysis of their reality, frequent use of the Scriptures, consideration of ecclesial documents, personal and communal prayer, formation-in-action processes, and Christian praxis.

In Covenant with God, like the rest of the books in the Builders of Hope series, is made up of five modules, which are described below. These modules are the initial journey, the first cycle of community meetings, the formation workshop, the second cycle of community meetings, and the retreat. The coordination of these modules is the responsibility of a coordinating team made up of three to five people. This team is selected from a group of people formed by the **animadores** of all the communities and two delegates previously selected by each community at the same level of formation.

The process in this book starts with a planning meeting. In this meeting, the coordinating team plans the initial journey, the community meetings, the formation workshop, and the retreat. A time line of the different modules appears on pages 14–15.

Description of the five modules

The following is a description of the five modules that make up the process of *In Covenant with God:*

Module 1: The initial journey

The initial journey offers the participants an experience of ecclesial community broader than that of their small communities, and helps them enter into the formation-in-action process. The initial journey may last one or two days, according to the judgment of the organizing team. The instructions for preparing the initial journey are found on pages 17–18.

Modules 2 and 4: The cycles of community meetings

Community meetings help the participants to live out a personal and communal Christian praxis in the church and society. The meetings are organized into two minicycles, each of which is made up of three or four meetings focused on themes related to the life of the participants, plus one meeting focused on the evaluation of the content and process of the previous meetings.

Each community should decide how frequently it will meet, taking into consideration its members' needs and commitments. The material designed for each meeting can be covered in one or two meetings, according to the situation of a given community. The important thing is to promote a more Christian life, adapting the materials as the community sees fit. In addition, a period of informal "hanging out" should always be included, as well as some time to discuss the community's shared life.

For each small community to have a life of its own, beyond the series of meetings outlined in this book, it is important that its members interact by calling one another on the telephone, visiting one another frequently, sharing pastoral and recreational activities, and regularly participating in the Eucharist as a community.

To prepare for these meetings and to know how to lead them, as well as to become familiar with their methodology, see the "Introduction: Community Meetings" on pages 30–33. If this material is used with people under sixteen years of age, it is recommended that it be adapted by dividing each community meeting into two sessions, so that the process can better meet the needs of this younger age-group.

Module 3: The formation workshop

The formation workshop is designed to occupy an entire day. Its objective is to allow members of various small communities to interact with one another and learn from trained professionals in areas demanding academic preparation, such as biblical **exegesis,** sociology, or educational theory. The workshop coordinating team is responsible for hiring the presenter well in advance to secure his or her availability. Additional instructions for preparing this workshop can be found on page 83.

Module 5: The retreat

The retreat offers the participants the opportunity to reflect more deeply on their faith experience—a process that they began during the initial journey and the community meetings. This will help them discern how their human development and Christian growth are proceeding. The retreat also celebrates the community's passage to the next stage of formation. It is recommended that members of various small communities that are at the same stage of formation participate together in the retreat so that they can exchange experiences and share a broader ecclesial encounter.

The retreat is designed to last a weekend. Friday's activities are intended for the participants from different communities to get to know one another and to create an appropriate ambience for the retreat; Saturday is reserved for reflection and prayer; and Sunday is devoted to sharing and celebrating the Eucharist. The coordinating team for the retreat is responsible for contacting a priest well in advance to secure his availability for the celebration of the Eucharist. Instructions for preparing the retreat are found on page 149.

Documents

The documents are informational articles that clarify aspects of faith frequently questioned or that require explanation to be understood. They serve as reference material for the general themes in the book and as resources for the formation workshop.

Appendices

Appendix 1, "Evaluation Forms," offers sample formats for preparing an evaluation for each of the modules. This evaluation of each of the modules in the process is very important for recognizing the contributions made by each module, for identifying those aspects that need improvement, and for fostering the maturation process of the participants and of the small communities.

Appendix 2 is a chart of the Witnesses of Hope collection. This chart presents the different series in the collection and explains the objectives of each book and its place in the Prophets of Hope process.

Note. The books in this series include the materials needed to design the initial journey, the community meetings, the formation workshop, and the retreat, in keeping with the methodology proposed here. Other resources are needed to help set the ambience for the meetings, to plan games, and to select songs.

Process and Scheduling:
In Covenant with God

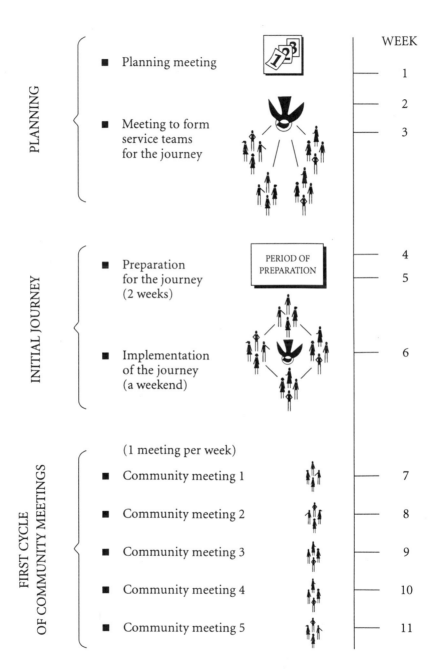

PLANNING

- Planning meeting

- Meeting to form service teams for the journey

INITIAL JOURNEY

- Preparation for the journey (2 weeks)

PERIOD OF PREPARATION

- Implementation of the journey (a weekend)

FIRST CYCLE OF COMMUNITY MEETINGS

(1 meeting per week)

- Community meeting 1
- Community meeting 2
- Community meeting 3
- Community meeting 4
- Community meeting 5

WEEK

1

2

3

4

5

6

7

8

9

10

11

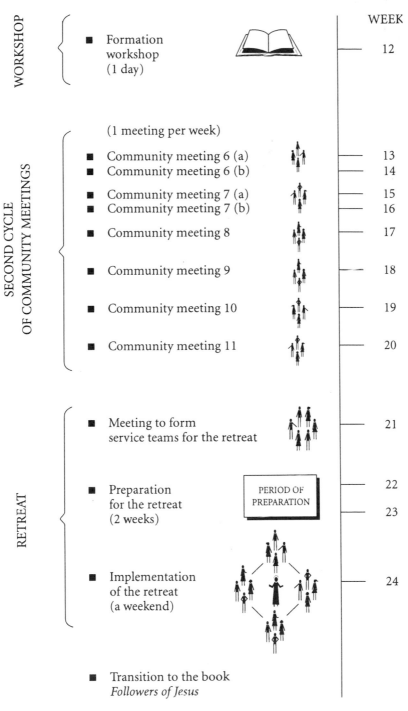

WORKSHOP

■ Formation
workshop
(1 day)

WEEK

12

SECOND CYCLE
OF COMMUNITY MEETINGS

(1 meeting per week)

■ Community meeting 6 (a)
■ Community meeting 6 (b)

■ Community meeting 7 (a)
■ Community meeting 7 (b)

■ Community meeting 8

■ Community meeting 9

■ Community meeting 10

■ Community meeting 11

13
14

15
16

17

18

19

20

RETREAT

■ Meeting to form
service teams for the retreat

21

■ Preparation
for the retreat
(2 weeks)

PERIOD OF
PREPARATION

22

23

■ Implementation
of the retreat
(a weekend)

24

■ Transition to the book
Followers of Jesus

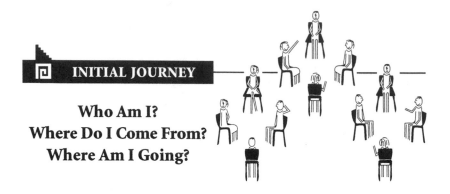

Who Am I?
Where Do I Come From?
Where Am I Going?

> Just as [God] chose us in Christ before the foundation of the world to be holy and blameless before him in love. [God] destined us for adoption as . . . children through Jesus Christ, according to the good pleasure of his will.
>
> —Ephesians 1:4–5

Overview

Objectives

- To reflect on our personal identity in light of our being a son or daughter of God
- To value ourselves as unique and irreplaceable persons, and to recognize the influences that have shaped our life
- To discover Jesus as a friend and guide who helps us know ourselves, forge our personalities, and grow in Covenant with God
- To discuss ways we can support one another in our faith journeys and in our efforts at personal development

Program

Introduction. Welcome, registration, singing, refreshments, opening prayer, and orientation (1 hour)

Icebreakers or warm-up activities (30 minutes)

Session 1: Created to live in Covenant with God (2 hours, 30 minutes)
A. Exercise: Engaging in a contract
B. Biblical circle: The nature of our Covenant with God
C. The comparison between God's Covenant with us
   and contracts between people

Session 2: Lifelines (2 hours)
A. Personal reflection
B. Reflection in community

Session 3: Visualizing our future as adults (1 hour, 30 minutes)
A. Interview
B. Personal reflection

Session 4: Persons fully alive (45 minutes)
A. Preparation of skits
B. Skits to be performed at one of the meals

Session 5: Liturgical celebration (45 minutes)
A. Meditation
B. Offertory procession
C. Final song

Session 6: Evaluation (45 minutes)

Preparation

The initial journey is intended for people who have committed themselves to continuing their Christian formation and to living within the context of a small community. The journey is planned as a weekend event; if it is to be done in a single day, adaptations will be needed. It is best if all the communities that are initiating this phase within a parish or diocese have this journey together. To prepare, first review the section, "Methodology of the Builders of Hope series," on pages 10–12, and then study the following process:

1. Planning meeting. The coordinating team, formed by the advisers, the *animadores,* and the community delegates, meets to plan the initial journey. This meeting should be held six weeks before the initial journey.

2. Meeting to form the service teams. The coordinating team and the members of the various communities get together two weeks before the initial journey to form a minimum of six basic service teams. The following is a list of the teams and their responsibilities:

- *The coordinating team* is responsible for the overall process of the initial journey.
- *The team of presenters and facilitators* is responsible for the different sessions.
- *The logistics team* is responsible for the facilities, the schedule, the meals, and all that concerns good order.
- *The pep team* is responsible for hospitality, games, and songs.
- *The liturgy team* is responsible for prayer and liturgical celebrations.
- *The evaluation team* is responsible for conducting and analyzing the evaluations.

It is important for *all* the people who plan to attend the initial journey to take part as a member of one of the service teams. Once the teams are formed, the members of each team elect a coordinator. This person is responsible for guiding the service team during the creation of a working plan and calendar, and for ensuring that the team members are prepared for, and take an active role in, the initial journey.

3. Preparation of the service teams. Each team holds the meetings it needs to prepare the service it will provide during the initial journey, according to the work plan and calendar.

4. Coordination meeting. The week before the initial journey, a meeting to coordinate the service teams and to make the necessary adjustments in the program should be held. People attending the meeting include the coordinating team and the coordinators of each of the service teams.

Session 1: Created to live in Covenant with God

A. Exercise: Engaging in a contract

1. Ask the participants to form an even number of groups of three to four people. Each group organizes itself to form a business partnership and then decides what kind of commercial business it will be and what the terms of the partnership will be. Write this information down in the contract for the partnership.

2. Each group of partners seeks out another group of partners with whom it can do some kind of commercial business. Both groups enter into negotiation. Together they write down what their deal will involve and the conditions under which they commit to carrying it out. They then close the deal and sign a contract.

3. Use the following questions to reflect on the exercise:
- What are the essential elements of a contract?
- What is needed to make a contract valid and for it to achieve the results for which it was designed?
- What happens when one party to a contract violates it, and what must be done to re-establish the agreement?

B. Biblical circle: The nature of our Covenant with God

Reflecting on the opening chapters of Genesis will help the participants understand the nature of God's Covenant with humanity. The Bible provides two Creation stories, arising from two different biblical traditions (see document 1, "How and Why the Bible Was Written," on pages 162–169). The first chapter of Genesis uses the form of a song to tell a solemn story of God's majestic act of Creation accomplished in a week's time through his great and all-powerful word. The second story, in the second chapter of Genesis, verses 4 to 25, recounts the Creation events in the style of a popular history.

In the same small groups in which the contract exercise took place, do the following:

1. Read and analyze chapter 1 of Genesis and Genesis 2:4–25 in order to answer the questions on page 21:

Act
of Incorporation
# of Partnership X

We: _____ , _____ ,
_____ , and _____
by virtue of the signatures appearing below,
declare that we have formed a commercial
partnership under the following conditions:

1.

2.

3.

Signature: _____ Signature: _____

Signature: _____ Signature: _____

Date: _____

- What qualities of God are revealed through these texts?
- What was God seeking when creating the universe and the human couple?
- How does the human couple relate to things created by God?

2. Read chapter 3 of Genesis. It tells of the expulsion of Adam and Eve from Paradise as a result of their sin. Paradise symbolizes the ideal state where human beings were called to live. Sin—breaking the Covenant of love with God—brings pain, sickness, and death as consequences.

- Analyze chapter 3 of Genesis by visualizing what it means to live in Covenant with God.
- Write down short phrases based on the reading that show what it would mean to live in Paradise nowadays.

3. Through the story of Cain, who kills his brother Abel, chapter 4 of Genesis illustrates the reality of how sin breaks the human relationships between us as brothers and sisters. Chapters 6 through 9 tell how God, on seeing the evil that exists between people, decides to re-establish the Covenant. The story of the flood, Noah's salvation, and God's promises to him convey the Israelites' conviction that God restored the Covenant through people who lived according to the plan of love.
Read Genesis 6:5–8,17–19; 8:14–22; and 9:1–3,8–17.

C. The comparison between God's Covenant with us and contracts between people

Compare and contrast the contracts made between people, with the Covenant that God makes with us, focusing on the following points:
- What are the historic circumstances that led to the signing of a contract and the establishment of the Covenant?
- Who are the contracting or covenanting parties?
- What is the objective of a contract and of the Covenant?
- What are the commitments made by both parties to a contract and to the Covenant?
- What are the similarities and differences in the written documents used in each of the cases?
- How are an agreement and the Covenant formalized?
- What are the reasons that a contract or the Covenant can be broken?
- How can a contract be renewed or the Covenant re-established?

Session 2: Lifelines

In this session we will try to gain deeper self-knowledge through personal meditation. Later we will share with others some aspects of our personal experience, so that we can become more fully aware of who we are as part of the **Hispanic** or **Latino** people of the United States and as part of the people of God.

Preparation. Have sheets of newsprint ready and titled with headings for each of the following groups: infancy, adolescence, and *juventud.* You will need red, green, black, yellow, brown, and blue markers.

A. Personal reflection

1. Devise a chart similar to the one on page 23 and draw a continuous line on it that represents your life experiences. Start with your childhood and continue through your present stage of life. Use the following signs:
- *an upward line* to indicate life stages or occasions of joy and happiness, or the achievement of some goal
- *a downward line* to indicate life stages or occasions of difficulty, failure, or disillusionment
- *a horizontal line* to indicate stages without special meaning
- *symbols* to represent triumphs, dreams, hopes, tragedies, and sorrows. For example, you might use a cross to indicate the death of someone you loved, an island might mean loneliness or isolation, or a candle might express new hope.

2. In the same chart, write key words that capture what happened in the different stages of your life. Use the following questions as a guide for your reflection:
- Who were the most significant persons at each stage of your life?
- What were your most important values at each stage? How have your values changed over time? Why have they changed?
- What experiences had the greatest impact on your life? Was that impact positive or negative? How did you handle these experiences?
- How was your relationship with God at each stage? How is it now?
- What attitudes and behaviors characterized your relations with other people during each stage?

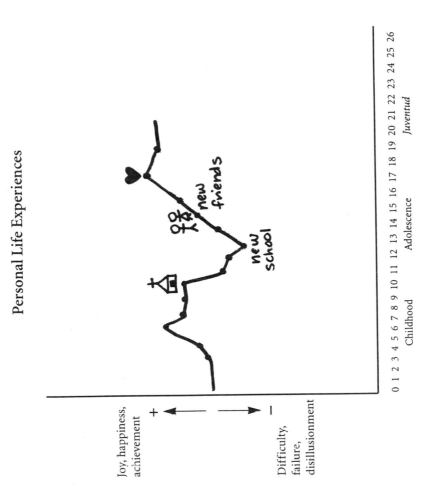

Personal Life Experiences

Joy, happiness, achievement +

← →

Difficulty, failure, disillusionment |

new friends

new school

0 1 2 3 4 5 6 7 8 9 10 11 12 13 14 15 16 17 18 19 20 21 22 23 24 25 26

Childhood   Adolescence   *Juventud*

B. Reflection in community

1. Each participant is to draw three symbols of the most meaningful moments of his or her life on a sheet of newsprint specially prepared for *all* the participants to use. The newsprint sheet should be taped to the wall. Before drawing the symbols, the participants should decide what stages of their life they will represent and which of the following symbols they will use:

a red heart to represent times of strength or stages of love or happiness

 a green smiling face for situations or times of hopes and dreams

 a black sad face for events or times that brought serious problems

 a yellow cross for events or periods of life that brought suffering or hurt

 a brown tornado for a crisis that separated you from God

 a blue upward arrow for a conversion that brought you closer to God

2. Invite the participants to come forward one at a time to draw their symbols on the newsprint sheets. When they are finished, ask the participants, in groups of three or four, to share the symbols they drew and explain what those symbols represent in their life, if they are comfortable doing so.

3. Have everyone observe one another's drawings. After a reasonable amount of time, initiate an open discussion to allow some of the participants to express the following:
- their personal experiences while doing the exercise
- their observations regarding what they saw on the newsprint and what was shared by their peers
- the implications for them that arise from gaining awareness of these aspects of their personal life and of the life of the other participants

Session 3: Visualizing our future as adults

Even though most of the members of the communities are already young adults, adult life extends far enough ahead for all the community members that we can consider it as belonging to the future. It is very important for them to imagine what they want to be and how they want to live their adult life. How they conduct their present life depends to a great extent on how they articulate and integrate these ideals. They will identify these ideals by visualizing their life when they are forty years old, using an exercise in which they pretend to be interviewed for a magazine.

A. Interview

Have the group form pairs, preferably joining participants who do not know each other well. Ask the pairs to take turns being the interviewer. Below are suggested questions that might be useful during the interview. Invite the participants to change or add questions.

The interviewer takes notes during the interview. Afterward each interviewer writes a paragraph describing what she or he heard the other say. Then the partners exchange paragraphs with each other and discuss what they wrote.

A guide for the interviews

Initiate the interview by reminding the participants that this dialog is happening when both of them are forty years old.

- How do you feel about having lived so long in the United States?
- Over the past twenty years, what have been your most significant personal achievements? professional achievements?
- On which aspects of your personality did you have to work most intently in order to become the mature person you are today?
- What have been the greatest contributions you have made to society?
- In what concrete ways has your faith in Jesus helped you?
- How has your participation in the Catholic church helped you to become who you are?

B. Personal reflection

- Correct or complete the sketch your partner made of you as a forty-year-old.
- Note three things about your life that you see more clearly as a result of the interview.
- Identify what attitudes, abilities, and qualities you need to develop in order to orient your life toward the purpose for which God created you.

Session 4: Persons fully alive

Through a skit with social content, the participants will try to represent persons who have fully realized their potential and can serve as models for their life. The skits can be presented during one of the meals, as if it were a dinner theater.

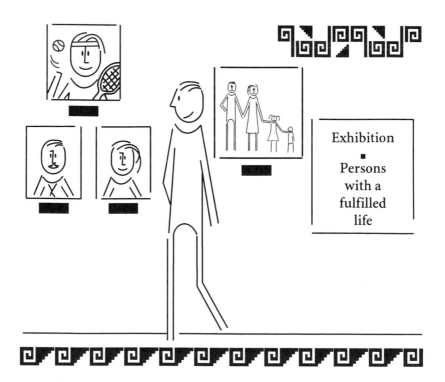

A. Preparation of skits

1. Form three or four groups. Each group member describes a person he or she admires and believes to be highly developed ethically and emotionally.

2. Each group then chooses one of the people discussed to present to the large group in its skit. The person most familiar with that individual becomes the principal actor; the others help in the skit.

3. Prepare the skit, demonstrating some of the model's personal attributes or aspects of her or his life. Make sure that everyone feels free to participate. Each skit should last 10 or 15 minutes, depending on how much time is available.

B. Skits to be performed at one of the meals

Session 5: Liturgical celebration

Preparation. Bring a Bible; a candle; a cross or crucifix; clay or ceramic cooking utensils, such as pots, pitchers, and vases; a small piece of modeling clay for each participant; and background music for the meditation.

A. Meditation

1. Arrange the chairs in a circle or semicircle, and place an altar in the center, using as the altar cloth the sheets of newsprint on which the participants recorded their life experiences. Place on the altar a Bible and the other things that you brought. Ask a person to prepare the reading from Jeremiah (18:1–8).

2. The facilitator gives each participant a piece of clay. Then he or she invites the participants to offer to God their life experiences and their commitment to take responsibility for their own personal development. The facilitator leads the following meditation, reading it aloud slowly:

> After having reflected on our personal history and on how we can further our human and Christian growth, we come together to celebrate God's marvelous work in each of our lives. Let us

place ourselves in God's presence and, in a spirit of prayer, allow the word of God to speak to our heart.

Read Jeremiah 18:1–8.

Close your eyes and feel the clay in your hands. Form it into a ball. This clay is a symbol of your life. Offer it up to God, asking God to transform you and give you new life. You must give God everything—all the good and the bad that has happened to you and that is within you, so that God can make a new creation.

Begin to shape the clay in a way that reflects your life. Recall the most difficult event you have remembered today, and how close or far off you felt God to be at that time. . . . Shape the clay according to how you felt: perhaps defeated, angry, powerless, lost. . . . Let your negative feelings find expression in the clay, and offer that experience up to God, so that you might be healed.

Now remember the happiest moment of your life, and give shape to how you felt: joyful, hopeful, full of love, full of life. . . . Think of how close God was during those moments. . . . Let your feelings of gratitude flood your spirit. . . . Offer your gratitude to God.

Now think of your present life. How do you feel in this stage of your life? Give shape to yourself by projecting onto the clay what is happening to you now; mold the clay to express your current situation. . . . Express the positive things in your life. . . . Express the challenges that you must confront. . . . Express the difficult or sorrowful aspects of your life, . . . your ideals and hopes. . . . Return to the memories or feelings that were most meaningful to you during this meditation, and work with them a bit longer. Speak to yourself about what you yearn for or about what worries you, placing all this in God's hands.

Think about your immediate future. What kind of person would you like to become? What graces do you want to ask God to give you? Give your future to God. . . . Take responsibility for it. What do you need to do? What habits and attitudes must you change? . . . What gifts must you develop? . . . Imagine yourself walking hand in hand with God, drawing from God's strength and love for you, and trusting that God will help you develop fully as his daughter or son. . . . Feel your calmness and happiness. God is with each of us. Amen.

B. Offertory procession

After some moments of silence, invite the participants to place their clay images at the foot of the cross or crucifix as a symbol of giving their life to God so that they may be transformed into new creations. As they are coming forward, one person reads slowly and with devotion Psalm 139: "O LORD, you have searched me and know me . . ."

C. Final song

Close with an offertory song or a song expressing trust in God.

Session 6: Evaluation

In order to do the written evaluation, use the form designed for the initial journey, which can be found in appendix 1, "Evaluation Forms," on pages 180–181. This form can be photocopied and duplicated. Give the participants twenty minutes to fill out the written portion of the evaluation. Then facilitate a twenty-five-minute session in which the participants share their responses.

Community Meetings

All community members are responsible for the life of the community. The ***animador/a*** cultivates the **communitarian** spirit and co-responsibility of the members, and supports and encourages them to continue forward during their faith journey. This person does not take on the role of **coordinator** or **facilitator** during meetings. Each meeting should have a coordinator who organizes and maintains order during the meeting, and who asks two other community members to serve as facilitators, one for the reflections and one for the prayers. The functions of coordination and facilitation rotate among all the members of the community as an expression of each person's commitment to the community. To further understand these roles, see document 2, "Roles in the Small Communities of *Jóvenes*," in *The Prophets of Hope Model*.

Each meeting discussed in this book is centered around a theme. The meeting theme can be divided into two meetings with the opening prayer, the life experience, and one commentary in one session, and the other commentary and the celebration of faith in the second session. Some part of the theme can also be postponed for a more in-depth discussion at a later date. If a given theme extends over several meetings, the coordinator may ask a community member to prepare a prayer to begin and end each meeting.

Methodology of the meetings

The meetings follow a methodology in which *all* the members of the small community enter into dialog and participate actively. The components that make up the majority of the meetings and that promote this participation are described on the following pages.

Opening prayer

The goal of the opening prayer is to help the participants become aware of God's presence and to ask God to help them live the Gospel. Each meeting includes suggestions for beginning the prayer, which then is followed by spontaneous prayer from any members of the community who wish to share a special intention.

The person facilitating the prayer prepares to do so through personal prayer and study of the biblical text and the content offered for the meeting. During the prayer, the facilitator encourages spontaneous prayer from community members. To help create the environment of prayer, the facilitator can play meditative music and bring objects related to the day's topic, such as pictures, flowers, or symbols.

Life experience

The life experience of the participants is the point of departure for their reflections. It helps them to assimilate the message of the meeting and to see clearly the relationship between their faith and their life. This part of the meeting consists of a shared activity that encourages interaction among the community members or helps them to understand their reality or a particular Gospel concept more deeply.

Illumination leading to action

Illumination leading to action occurs through two or three commentaries on different aspects of the participants' daily life or their faith. Each commentary contains reflection exercises to encourage a deepening of faith and questions that serve to guide the Christian praxis of the community. The commentaries can be prepared as a special presentation by one individual, read in silence by each member of the community, or read aloud by one person to the whole community.

Celebration of our faith

The celebration of our faith facilitates incarnation of the faith in the life of the participants by helping them discover and nourish the seed sown by God within their heart and mind during the meeting. It includes different kinds of prayer and makes use of symbols, rites, and songs. It also provides a time of silent prayer so that each person can meditate on the message received in the meeting and then write this message in the margins of this book or in a diary used for this purpose. These notes are key for carrying forward the process of faith formation and spiritual growth promoted by the Builders of Hope series.

Preparation for the meetings

It is important for the coordinator and facilitators to prepare themselves ahead of time. This preparation includes the following aspects:
*   *studying the theme* of the particular meeting, and adapting the material, if necessary, to make the meeting respond more directly to the needs of the community
*   *praying for the meeting* so that the Holy Spirit may guide the coordinator and facilitators in their preparations and leadership
*   *preparing the material* if the group dynamics or exercises require any special material or other prior preparations
*   *preparing the celebration of our faith* so that everything needed to create a prayerful setting is arranged, including selecting and preparing songs and symbols
*   *coordinating the meeting facilitation* so that each facilitator is familiar with the part of the meeting for which he or she is responsible

Evaluation and celebration of each cycle of meetings

It is recommended that the evaluation of each cycle of meetings be done at the end of that cycle in a special meeting designed for this purpose. Evaluation forms for each cycle of meetings can be found in appendix 1, "Evaluation Forms," on pages 182–183 and 186–187. These forms may be photocopied and duplicated to facilitate the collection and analysis of the data. Give the participants thirty minutes to fill out the written portion of the evaluation. Allow another thirty-minute session for the participants to share their responses.

All evaluation processes are opportunities for growth that we can respond to with God's grace and our own mutual support. To accomplish a good evaluation, a critical and positive attitude is necessary. First identify the areas where the community is doing well or improving. Then identify those areas that need work. Finally, outline the challenges the community seeks to address in the short term.

It is recommended that on the day of the evaluation, the community celebrate the end of the cycle of meetings with a social activity, like going out to a restaurant or a movie, or having a picnic.

Created in the Image and Likeness of God

So God created humankind in his image,
    in the image of God he created them;
    male and female he created them.
God blessed them, and God said to them, "Be fruitful and
multiply, and fill the earth and subdue it."

        —Genesis 1:27–28

Overview

Objectives

- To reflect on what it means to be a person
- To recognize that the Covenant with God is lived out within a community

Plan for the meeting

Opening prayer

Life experience: We discover who we are

Illumination leading to action
Commentary 1: What it means to be a person
Commentary 2: God's plan for humanity

Celebration of our faith: Giving thanks to God

Let's begin with a prayer

We bring ourselves into God's presence and in silence ask God to help us in this new cycle of our small community meetings. In these meetings we will deepen our understanding of what it means to have been created in God's image and likeness, and to live in Covenant with God and other people.

God is here among us to strengthen the Covenant with each of us present. Let us offer our life to God and ask the Holy Spirit to come among us. All are invited to share any prayers they feel moved to offer.

Life experience: We discover who we are

To begin our reflection, we enter into a meditation that will help us discover more about ourselves and help us better communicate with God. The facilitator invites the participants to get comfortable and explains what is coming. With music in the background, the facilitator reads the following in a tranquil and soothing voice, pausing between each bulleted section:

• Listen to your breathing. Feel how the air enters into you. Every time your breath leaves you, think of your name and repeat it silently to yourself.
• Listen to the beating of your heart, and feel the blood flowing through your body. Think about the love and affection you are able to give and receive.

- Mentally touch each part of your body, beginning with your feet, . . . then your legs, . . . your stomach, . . . your arms, . . . your hands, . . . your chest, . . . your head, . . . your eyes, . . . your mouth. . . . Thank God for each of these parts and for your whole body.
- Think of yourself as a man or a woman. Bless God for the beauty of your gender. Think of all your gifts and qualities as a male or female . . . and how they allow you to collaborate in God's creation and plan of salvation.
- Focus again on your head, and cherish your desire and capacity for knowledge, reflection, and analysis. Now feel the passions of your heart, and recognize your desire and your capacity to love and to be loved.
- Repeat in silence: "This person, with these desires and capacities, is me. I do not live alone, but rather with other people who have desires and abilities similar to mine."
- We exist in the midst of many people, in an immense world, and at times we feel like we have lost ourselves and no longer know who we are.
- In this world, many animals, plants, rivers, mountains, and valleys also exist. Think of the natural setting in which you feel most at home, perhaps on a beach by the sea, . . . on top of a mountain, . . . in a forest, . . . by a river. . . . Imagine yourself there, and relax as you savor the moment.
- What do you see there? . . . Who would you like to have with you? . . . What would you like to hear them say? . . . What do you want to say to them?

- Look at their faces . . . and the way they look back at you. Feel their love. How do they make you feel? . . . How do you make them feel? . . . What does each of them ask of you? . . . What does each offer to you?
- Rest, . . . listen to the music, . . . breathe deeply, one . . . two . . . three times. Breathe deeply again. When you breathe out, repeat your name in silence.
- You are a unique and irreplaceable person. God has not made anyone else quite like you. . . . Nobody is quite like you. . . . You are you, . . . only you, and you are created in the image and likeness of God.
- Within this community, . . . among the people who love you, . . . of all the people around you, . . . you stand out. You are different. You have your own history, . . . your own ideals, . . . your own thoughts, . . . your own feelings. . . . You are responsible for your own life. No one can take from you the freedom to be yourself.
- Go back to being alone. Are you at peace? . . . Rest. Let your muscles relax. . . . God is with you. . . . God gives you life, . . . loves you, . . . whispers in your ear. . . . What does God say to you? . . . Who are you in God's sight? . . . Who is God in your life?
- Place yourself in front of God, your creator and the creator of the universe. Remain there, and look in God's eyes. Who are you?
- What does God want to say to you? To what does God call you?
- What do you want to ask from God? What do you want to offer to God?
- Listen to the music. . . . Take delight in the marvelous person that you are. . . . Give thanks for your life and for the people who are important to you.
- Breathe deeply. Say your name silently. Think about where you are. . . . Think of the others at this meeting as your companions on the great journey and adventure of being you, . . . of being important, . . . of every day developing more and more as a person.
- Open your eyes and look at your companions. Feel what it is like to be together. Get up slowly. Join hands and form a circle.
- Think about your individuality. . . . Yet in your solitude you have company, for God created us as beings in community.

- In this spirit of community, share with one another the experience you had during this meditation.

Reflection

1. In groups of four, share your answers to the following questions:
- How did you feel during the meditation? What moment during the reflection do you remember most intensely?
- What did you learn about yourself?

2. Share your answer to the following question with the whole small community:
- What new horizons did this meditation open up for you?

Illumination leading to action

The meditation helped us discover something new about ourselves. Now, through the commentaries, we will have the opportunity to deepen our knowledge of some aspects of our human nature.

Commentary 1: What it means to be a person

To be a person is to be capable of dreaming and questioning, enjoying and suffering, laughing and crying. It means being able to be in contact with ourselves in the silence of our heart, and being able to relate to other people and other beings in God's creation. It is having the power to create and to transform, to destroy and to corrupt. It is being able to love and to suffer from lack of love; to hold knowledge and to remain in ignorance. Human beings have almost infinite capacity, both for good and for evil. The answers we give to the following questions regarding our life profoundly influence how we use these abilities:
- Who am I?
- Why and for what purpose was I born?
- Who do I want to become?
- What meaning does my life hold?
- What do the lives of all the people around me mean?
- What meaning does God have in my life?

What we think about ourselves and other persons, how we feel, and how we act depend to a great extent on how we respond to these questions. Many young people ask themselves these things only after they find themselves in situations that they do not understand or that cause them great pain. To find answers that satisfy us, we must look at our experiences and reflect on them clearly and consciously.

Reflection
- Do the following personal reflection: Of the six questions on page 38, choose the most important one for you at this stage in your life. Respond to it briefly in writing.
- Share your personal reflections in groups of three, explaining why you chose this question and how you responded to it.

Called to live the Gospel
To what kind of action are we called as members of the community by having become more aware of the meaning of our human existence?

Commentary 2: God's plan for humanity

God's plan is for all of humanity to live as brothers and sisters. All human beings were created, born, and have life because God loves us. God created all of us in his image and likeness as the fruit of love, and God calls us to live in Covenant with him and with other people. The life of each person is part of God's plan for humanity, and each one of us is a member of God's family or the people of God.

Beyond life itself, the greatest gifts God has given us are our freedom, our sense of justice, and our capacities to love, to think, and to decide. Our happiness and the happiness of those who share in our life depend on how we use these gifts.
- *God's plan is that we have freedom.* To the extent that we are free, we can choose well, seek justice, and decide according to God's will.
- *God's plan is that we have a sense of justice.* We will seek the common good with a preferential option for the poor, the marginalized, and the oppressed.
- *God's plan is that we love ourselves and others.* If we love ourselves and one another, society will function with justice and peace.

- *God's plan is that we use our capacities for knowledge and reason.* If we discover the truth about God, ourselves, and our world, we will find joy.
- *God's plan is that we live in harmony.* If we live harmoniously in relationship with God and those around us, we will grow as persons.

Being a person implies the ability to live in relation with God, with other persons, with the world around us, and with ourselves. As Christians we live in communion of love with the Holy Trinity—with God, as his daughters and sons; with Jesus, as his disciples, sisters, and brothers; and with the Holy Spirit, as the source of all love and truth. This participation in God's love helps us to relate

- to ourselves, as persons of great dignity who embody a marvelous life project
- to others, as brothers and sisters, children of the same God
- to nature and the good things we produce, as stewards charged with caring for them and using them for the good of all humanity

What We Are and What We Are Not

We are the "summit" of creation,
with great responsibility for ourselves
and for the rest of creation.
We were created to be sisters and brothers together,
to collaborate with God in his creative work,
and to share the good things of creation.
We are not quasi-gods or owners of the universe.

We are sons and daughters of God,
worthy of being valued and respected.
We were created with great dignity.
We are proud of that dignity and we will defend it.
We are not trash, neither insignificant nor inferior to others.

We are transcendent beings,
each with a soul or vital center
that allows us to love God and to love other people.
We were created to live a spiritual life.
We are not robots, who depend ultimately on material things
      or technology.

We are free,
with freedom to love and to choose
how we want to be and what we want to do.
We were created as agents of history
to build a society of love, justice, and peace.
We are not objects, nor do we allow ourselves to be manipulated.

We are part of a people.
We were born into a specific nation, culture, and historical age.
We were created to live with other persons
and in solidarity with all humanity.
We are not isolated beings, marginalized or guided by egoism.

Reflection
- What does this poem say about human dignity? As Christians, what do we need to do to live according to God's plan?
- What does being free imply for our life? How can we make better use of our freedom, so that we live in Covenant with God and with others?

• What experiences tend to be lived in isolation and motivated by egoism? In what ways do you demonstrate your solidarity with other persons?

Called to live the Gospel

In what ways is it urgent that we, as community members, change our way of living and acting, so that we can live according to God's plan? Brainstorm some needed changes, and then decide on one or two changes that the community will try to accomplish.

Celebration of our faith: Giving thanks to God

1. During this meeting we have deepened our understanding of the glories and responsibilities of being human. Together we are going to write a psalm; later we will pray it together as a community. Psalms are songs from the Bible, each made up of short stanzas. Step 4 presents several opening lines for stanzas that should be completed with a partner.

The community should be broken into pairs. Each set of partners is assigned a stanza to complete. If there are not enough stanzas, begin again with the first one.

2. Each pair writes their stanza on newsprint in large letters so that everyone can read it. The stanzas are then taped to the wall to complete the psalm.

3. An altar, with a candle and a Bible, should be set up in front of the wall. When all is ready, the facilitator begins the prayer by inviting everyone to enter into God's presence. The psalm is prayed by dividing the community into two choruses—left and right—that take turns reciting the stanzas written by the participants.

4. Pray the following psalm:

Facilitator
Our Father, we are proud
and thankful for being your sons and daughters.
We praise you, we bless you, and we give you thanks
for the life that you give us.

Left
Lord, giver of life, we thank you because . . .

Right
We want to glorify you because . . .

Left
We bless you because . . .

Right
We ask your help so that . . .

Left
We place ourselves into your hands so that . . .

Right
We want to be a community that . . .

Left
Bless us so that we can . . .

Right
We need special grace so that . . .

Left
Remember all those young people who . . .

Right
We pray for all those young people who . . .

Facilitator
You have spoken to our heart,
and we have heard your voice.
Help us to respond to your love
and every day become better persons. Amen.

Take a moment to listen to what God wants to say to each of us, in light of the message of this meeting. Write in your book or diary a few phrases that remind you of God's words.

Take turns hugging each other or offering each other a sign of peace, celebrating the greatness of being human and the opportunity to grow as persons.

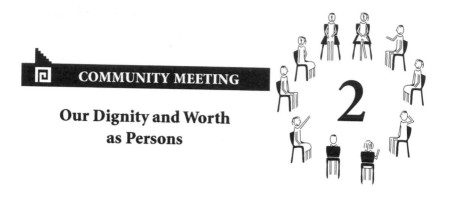

COMMUNITY MEETING

Our Dignity and Worth
as Persons

Blessed be the God and Father of our Lord Jesus Christ, who has blessed us in Christ with every spiritual blessing in the heavenly places. . . . [God] destined us for adoption as his children through Jesus Christ, according to the good pleasure of his will.

—Ephesians 1:3–5

Overview

Objectives

- To discover ways to strengthen our self-esteem
- To recognize that our worth as persons has its foundation in God
- To become aware of what helps and hinders us in valuing ourselves

Plan for the meeting

Opening prayer

Life experience: I am pulled in many directions

Illumination leading to action
Commentary 1: How to strengthen self-esteem
Commentary 2: Overcoming prejudices and stereotypes
Commentary 3: Jesus and Mary teach us to value ourselves

Celebration of our faith: Surrender and liberation

Let's begin with a prayer

In the previous meeting, we reflected on our likeness to God and our nature as communitarian beings called to live in Covenant with God and our brothers and sisters. Today we will see how our worth and dignity as persons are founded in God. Let us begin by praying Psalm 8. All respond, "How majestic is your name in all the earth!"
- Everyone prays the responsorial psalm, repeating the response after each stanza. Different people take turns praying the stanzas.
- The prayer is then opened to community members who wish to add their own spontaneous prayers.

Life experience: I am pulled in many directions

Preparation. The facilitator asks three participants to prepare the role-play ahead of time.

The scene begins with three people standing up. The middle person holds hands with the other two. The person in the middle will be pulled alternately to each side, as the other two say positive or negative things about him or her, about young people in general, about Hispanics, or about Hispanic culture. The person on the left side will say negative things while pulling the middle person's arm downward. Particularly negative statements should come with an exaggerated downward tug. The person on the right will say positive things and pull that arm upward. The "tugs" should be rather gentle, but they do not need to alternate evenly; sometimes two positive or negative things can be said consecutively, so that one arm is pulled twice in a row. The following are some examples of positive and negative ideas:

Negative Ideas	Positive Ideas
Hispanics are very lazy.	If you try, you'll succeed.
Young people are a waste.	Your friendship helps me.
I wish you were like your brother or sister.	The group needs you.
Hispanics are ignorant and have awful taste.	Hispanic young people give us hope and joy.

1. Carry out the dramatization.

2. Reflect together on the following topics:
- In what ways do you identify with each of the people involved in the role-play?
- Share how some of the attitudes or actions of others have had a positive influence on your self-esteem, and some ways in which you have exercised that positive influence on others.
- Share some of the attitudes or actions of others that have had a negative influence on your self-esteem, and discuss how they have affected you.

Illumination leading to action

The role-play showed how other people influence the way we see ourselves, in both positive and negative ways. The following commentaries will help us to base our self-worth in God and to learn ways to develop our self-esteem.

Commentary 1: How to strengthen self-esteem

Valuing ourselves is crucial for our personal development, our participation in society, and our collaboration in building the Reign of God. Self-esteem is based on our awareness of God's love for us, our own self-acceptance and self-love, and the realization that others value us for who we are. To strengthen our self-esteem, we need to love ourselves, respect ourselves, and feel secure and confident in ourselves. The following reflections can help us in this process:

1. *Loving ourselves.* Self-love is based in the experience of being loved and being able to love others. When we have been loved by our family, it is easier for us to love. But a lack of love in our family does not mean that we cannot learn to love, for we can encounter the love of God through prayer, as well as in the love of other people.

2. *Respecting ourselves.* Self-respect comes from the interior conviction that we are sons and daughters of God and that, as such, we are fundamentally good. Our attraction to evil does not alter our essential goodness, but rather reflects the freedom that we have to act in facing life's challenges and the limitations of human nature.

When we consider something to be good, authentic, beautiful, or useful, we respect it. But when we think of something as bad, fake, ugly, or useless, we tend to squander it. Love and respect for ourselves make us treat our own life with care, as well as make us refuse to allow others to do us damage. Those who internalize negative images of themselves tend to put themselves down or allow others to do so. They often act in a manner that denies their own dignity, and they often dedicate themselves to pursuing pleasure without regard for their dignity as God's children. They may even try to evade reality through drugs.

3. Having confidence in ourselves. Self-confidence develops when we recognize our ability to make the right decisions and carry them out. The way our mind and heart work within us is both great and terrifying. We are capable of great achievements, and we have serious deficiencies. Recognizing our potential and accepting our limitations gives us a balanced vision of what we are, free of exaggerated illusions and defeatist pessimism.

4. Feeling secure in who we are. Feeling secure is demonstrated by expressing firmly our ideals and needs, with clarity and without fear; by struggling to achieve our goals without feeling defeated by obstacles; by striving steadfastly to satisfy our needs; and by developing the abilities and seeking out the resources we need to achieve our ideals.

When we value ourselves, we can treat other people as equals and receive their criticism in a positive spirit, making use of it for our personal growth. Furthermore, self-esteem allows us to take the initiative to achieve our ideals, embrace our responsibilities, resolve our conflicts, and stand up for our rights. We love with greater authenticity, without worrying about pleasing other people in ways that belittle our culture, personality, ideals, values, and development.

Reflection

1. Form four groups. Each group reflects on one of the four elements needed to strengthen self-esteem—love, respect, confidence, and security in ourselves—by doing the following:
- Name some concrete ways this Christian community has helped you increase your self-esteem.
- Share the greatest challenges to your ability to love, respect, have confidence, and feel secure in yourself.

2. Share your group's reflections on these issues with the whole community.

Called to live the Gospel
- Identify some ways you can help one another as a community to grow in self-esteem through love, respect, self-confidence, and security in yourselves.
- Identify some ways you can help other young people bolster their self-esteem. Make a commitment to help them.

Commentary 2: Overcoming prejudices and stereotypes

Prejudices and stereotypes make it difficult for people to respect, trust, and love one another. *Prejudices* consist of judging people or their actions while ignoring the reasons and circumstances that explain their behavior. *Stereotypes* are concepts that represent an oversimplified opinion, a prejudiced attitude, or a subjective judgment about a person or a social group. In general, prejudices and stereotypes are

- born of perceptions that do not objectively correspond to reality
- rationalizations generated to support one's ideology or personal antipathies
- ways of characterizing and placing others in set categories according to preconceived images
- self-defense mechanisms created by people and institutions in order to evade or manipulate reality and to excuse their failure to change hurtful attitudes and behaviors

When prejudices affect the impartiality of the law and other social structures, we speak of institutionalized prejudices. These prejudices cause racism, ethnocentrism, classism, sexism, discrimination, or marginalization.

Racism is an attitude of believing that one race is genetically superior to others. *Ethnocentrism* is the conviction that one ethnic group is more valuable and embodies more positive qualities than other ethnic groups. *Classism* consists of prejudging or discriminating against people on the basis of their belonging to a particular social class. *Sexism* involves prejudging or discriminating against people based on their gender. *Discrimination* is to differentiate in the treatment given to other people by considering them inferior. It occurs when persons or social groups are categorized according to their differences, and those categorizations become the basis for ignoring their human rights or excluding them from participating in particular social structures. *Marginalization* is the lack of integration of people, social groups, or communities into the full life of the society in which they live.

To better live out our Covenant with God and with our brothers and sisters, it is necessary to overcome the effects of the types of destructive attitudes previously mentioned. Some of the ways this can be done are as follows:

- by cultivating and developing a greater awareness of being daughters and sons of God through meditation on the Gospel
- by talking with people of faith, and by engaging in personal and communal prayer
- by treating one another like brothers and sisters, without making distinctions of gender, race, nationality, social class, or religious tradition
- by analyzing the destructive powers of each of the attitudes presented here and their effects on our life and the lives of others
- by dialoging and collaborating with persons from social or cultural groups different than our own

Reflection

1. Form two groups. One of the groups analyzes the prejudices or stereotypes that have affected their self-esteem most negatively. The other group focuses on their own prejudices or stereotypes toward other ethnic groups, social classes, or persons of the other sex.

- Brainstorm ideas and write them down on a sheet of newsprint.
- Choose the most commonly shared prejudices or stereotypes, or those that cause the most harm. Analyze their origin and their effects on young people.

2. Share your ideas of how to overcome prejudices with the whole community.

Called to live the Gospel

What actions can we take as a community to help other young people strengthen their sense of self-worth?

Commentary 3:
Jesus and Mary teach us to value ourselves

This commentary is based on a reflection on two passages from the Gospels that show the attitudes of Jesus and Mary toward themselves and others. Both Jesus and Mary recognized God as Father and considered themselves loved in a very special way by God. They exhibited self-confidence, and they accepted their mission with conviction. At the same time, they did all this with humility and fortitude. True humility leads us to recognize that everything good that we are and that we have comes from God. Valuing ourselves with humility helps us to identify the gifts God has given us and to use them to face life with an authentic Christian spirit.

Reflection

1. Divide the community into two or four groups, depending on its size. Give each group a number from one to four. Assign the two passages given below so that half of the participants read the first passage and the other half read the second passage. Have one person in each group read aloud the assigned passage. Afterward direct the group to discuss the passage in light of the given questions.

Reading and questions for groups 1 and 3: Luke 1:46–55
- What are the noble feelings that Mary is expressing? What type of feelings do you have?
- What makes Mary happy? What reasons do you have to give thanks to God?

- How does Mary see herself in the history of her people? What mission do you have in the history of the Hispanic people in the United States?

Reading and questions for groups 2 and 4: Matthew 11:25–30
- Who does Jesus love and value? Why?
- Who is valued by society in general? Who do you love and value?
- Who is Jesus concerned about? Who are you concerned about?
- How is Jesus a refuge for the oppressed? How do you help those who are oppressed?

2. Form new pairs or groups of four, bringing together participants who read the different passages to share their reflections.

Called to live the Gospel
Identify a characteristic of Jesus or Mary that all of you would like to cultivate. Share some ideas of how you can support one another in this effort.

Celebration of our faith: Surrender and liberation

1. The facilitator invites the community members to form a circle and hold hands in a spirit of prayer. He or she plays background music and begins the prayer, allowing enough time between each question so the participants can pray after each one is posed.

2. The facilitator invites the community members to take part in a prayer in which they will incorporate their personal reflections by offering to God the oppressions, worries, and hopes that were brought to light during the course of this meeting.

Facilitator: Remember the role-play, "I am pulled in many directions," and imagine yourself as the person in the middle. From what influences or negative concepts do you need to free or liberate yourself in order to strengthen your self-esteem? I invite you to pray aloud, asking the Lord for his strength. Our response will be, "Free us from this bondage."

Spontaneous prayer

Facilitator: As a sign of liberation from these negative ties, raise your hands toward God. What positive feelings, gifts, and qualities do you need to develop in order to increase your self-esteem? Let us pray, thanking the Lord for these gifts. Our response will be, "We thank you for these blessings."

Spontaneous prayer

Facilitator: As a sign of the strength that the community's prayers give us, let us hold hands again. On what do you base your self-esteem? Let us pray, asking Mary to teach us to purify our heart of all feelings of mediocrity. Our response will be, "Mary, teach us to be like you."

Spontaneous prayer

Facilitator: As a sign of our willingness to accept and develop the gifts God has given us, we reach forward, with our palms turned upward. How can you follow Jesus' model in your relationship with other people? Let us pray, asking Jesus to help us to be good disciples. Our response will be, "We trust in you; give us your light and your strength."

Spontaneous prayer

Facilitator: We end the prayer with a sign that we are a community of Jesus' disciples, sharing Christ's peace with one another and saying, "God's love and strength be with you," to which the response is, "And also with you."

3. Take a moment to listen to what God wants to tell each one of us, in light of this meeting's message. Then write in your book or diary some of the phrases that will remind you of God's words.

4. Close with a song that speaks of liberation.

We Grow in Community

All who believed were together and had all things in common; they would sell their possessions and goods and distribute the proceeds to all, as any had need.

—Acts of the Apostles 2:44–45

Overview

Objectives

- To become aware of our need for belonging and love
- To discover the importance of the community in enabling us to grow as persons

Plan for the meeting

Opening prayer

Life experience: Well-being, community, and maturity

Illumination leading to action
Commentary 1: Our need for belonging and love
Commentary 2: Personal growth and its communitarian dimension
Commentary 3: Human development

Celebration of our faith: We share like brothers and sisters

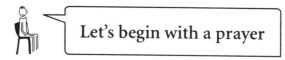

Let's begin with a prayer

In the previous meeting, we reflected on our dignity and worth as persons. Now we will reflect on our need for belonging, love, and personal development. We will begin by meditating on Acts of the Apostles 2:44–45, which demonstrates the ideal for a Christian community. Let us take careful notice of every word, allowing it to echo to the bottom of our heart.

• One person reads the whole passage.
• Different people take turns reading a clause, leaving a moment of silence between each one: "All who believed . . . were together . . . and had all things in common; . . . they would sell their possessions and goods . . . and distribute the proceeds to all, . . . as any had need."
• Some participants share the messages they received while in prayer. Then two or three participants pray in the name of the community.

Life experience: Well-being, community, and maturity

1. Form three groups. Have each group work together to resolve the following case:

As a community, you have decided to adopt three siblings who were orphaned when their parents were killed in an automobile accident. The children are four, six, and twelve years old. Organize and assign roles among yourselves to secure the general well-being, education, and economic future of the children. Take into consideration the needs of each child and the resources that each member of the community has for responding to those needs.

2. Share with the whole community the way you organized yourselves.

3. Reflect in community on what you learned through this activity.

Illumination leading to action

The activity we have just finished demonstrates the need we have for one another and shows that when we get organized and work together, we not only help ourselves but we also help others. The commentaries presented here will allow us to look more deeply into the importance of communitarian development in achieving our personal development.

Commentary 1: Our need for belonging and love

All human beings have a need for belonging and love. When God created us, God created us out of love and invited us to belong to God, along with the rest of God's sons and daughters, in order to form a vast united human family. Each time we interrupt this communion of love by sin, we need to repent our actions so as to reconcile ourselves with God and each other, thereby re-establishing our communion with God and reincorporating ourselves into God's family.

The small community is a privileged environment where we can live in love and achieve a sense of belonging. From this experience we are better prepared to offer love to other people and to help them feel part of a society that accepts them and gives them a part in making history. The following comments will help in our reflections:

The need for belonging. The need for belonging is vital during our childhood and adolescence, but remains important throughout our life. As children, it is important for us to have a family in which we are loved and cared for. As young people, it is key that we belong to a group of friends. We all need a social environment in which we are accepted, respected, and valued for who we are. These needs correspond to our social nature, which desires shared living and understanding in order to live happily and grow as persons. Furthermore, we need to be accepted in the social settings where we spend our time: for example, among classmates and work companions, as well as in broader settings, such as the neighborhood, government offices, schools, and medical clinics.

The meaning of belonging has two dimensions. On one hand, we need to feel secure about our place in the group and to participate actively in its activities. On the other hand, the group needs to accept us, recognize our gifts, and give us a role in its activities.

The need for love. Love is often expressed through tenderness, warmth, and affection. This leads to a desire for psychological and spiritual intimacy, and in the case of some relationships, its also leads to a yearning for physical intimacy. The need for love has two dimensions: to love and to be loved.

People who love give the same importance to fulfilling the needs of the people they love as they do to fulfilling their own needs. To love is to affirm the self and individuality of the loved one and to seek actively his or her well-being and personal development. It leads to care, responsibility, and concern for others. It leads to accepting others as they are, respecting their individuality and personality, and sharing in their joys and sorrows, triumphs and defeats.

Love begets love. The fuller the love between two people, then the freer their relationship: the more they can love other people fully, and the more that love will increase their mutual love. It is very important for society to understand the meaning of love and to be able to grow in it and express it. Families and small communities are privileged seedbeds for love.

Reflection

1. Identify several ways you experience a feeling of belonging in your small community.

2. List the types of attitudes and acts with which you demonstrate love to your peers in the community, and state what you can do to help everyone feel a part of the community.

3. Identify some attitudes or acts that demonstrate a lack of love toward one another or that prevent everyone from becoming fully integrated into the community.

Called to live the Gospel

1. On a sheet of newsprint, draw a large circle to symbolize the community.

2. Ask each participant to draw himself or herself inside the circle, and to draw one arrow facing in toward the drawing of himself or herself, and one facing out toward the circle. On the arrow pointing in, tell the participant to write a word that indicates how the community can give love and foster the feeling of belonging. On the arrow pointing out, have the participant indicate a way he or she can give love and foster the feeling of belonging.

3. Have all the participants look over the circle carefully, and then ask them to talk about God's call to them as a community.

Commentary 2:
Personal growth and its communitarian dimension

Personal growth implies the development of our abilities and qualities, the search for truth and for what is good, the creation of beauty, the growth of a spirituality, the elaboration of a life project, and the promotion of justice. All of this supposes a continual growth process, with both a personal and a communitarian dimension.

The community—be it the family, a group of friends, the small ecclesial community, the school, or other instances of community—is one of the most fitting environments and vehicles for orienting and nurturing the personal growth process. Shortly we will see four categories of needs we have to satisfy if we want to achieve personal growth. The reflection exercise that follows will allow us to understand the role of the community in our personal development.

Interpersonal communication needs. Interpersonal communication needs arise from our yearning to express our feelings and thoughts, to be understood and to understand, and to dialog to clarify our perceptions. Without interpersonal communication we close ourselves off to the world and marginalize ourselves, shortchanging ourselves the richness that other people can bring to us with their experiences and wisdom.

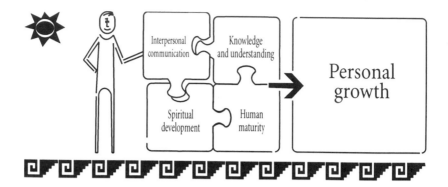

The need for knowledge and understanding. We need to understand the world and to know truth in its various dimensions. These dimensions include the need to think, to continue one's education, to reflect, to reason, to analyze, and to resolve conflicts, as well as the need to communicate at the interpersonal and social levels. The development of these abilities facilitates our maturation process and helps us manage properly the reality in which we live in order to achieve our personal well-being and the common good.

Spiritual needs. Spiritual needs are related to our search for purpose and meaning in our life as human beings. These needs also concern our search for values and for expressions of our spiritual dimension through art, philosophy, and religion. Our spiritual needs lead us to search for God, to expand our horizons, and to bring about the transformation of society for the benefit of humanity.

Maturation needs. Maturation needs refer to the potential every human being has to develop all of her or his abilities to the fullest. Personal maturation leads us to consider the well-being of others as a priority; to focus our life on noble and just causes; to live intensely, enjoying God's creation with a sense of unity with nature; to be open, honest, and sincere persons; to act according to our convictions; to accept changes that lead to a better world; and to always face life with hope.

The mature person has his or her basic needs for security and self-esteem met, and knows how to receive and give love. This allows the person to leave the egocentric self behind and dedicate himself or herself to serving others, to searching for truth in unknown and unexplored areas, and to creating art or performing life-giving deeds for other people.

Reflection

1. Reflect personally on each of the four categories of needs presented and then do the following: *(a)* rank them according to how important they are for you to work on at this stage of your life, and *(b)* think about how you can better meet the two types of needs you rated most important.

• In what ways can you work on these needs in your everyday life?
• How can the community help you?

2. Bring your personal reflections to the whole community. Post a sheet of newsprint with a column assigned to each of the four types of needs. Invite each participant to state her or his two top needs in order of importance. As the needs are being said, mark the most important need with two crosses and the second most important need with one cross. At the end, tally up the crosses. The category of needs with the greatest number of crosses is the most important one for the community.

Called to live the Gospel

Observe what was indicated on the newsprint. Think together about what you each need to do individually for your community to be a source of personal development and growth for all. Give a few concrete ideas based on your personal reflections.

Commentary 3: Human development

In his encyclical letter *On the Development of Peoples (Populorum Progressio)*, Pope Paul VI says that in order for persons to achieve full human development, they must become more human each day. To accomplish this, people must work to meet their basic needs, to develop their mind through study, and to expand their heart through relationships of love. The most certain way of achieving personal growth is through our relationship with God and with others.

Note. One person reads aloud the following text of the encyclical letter, *Populorum Progressio,* of Pope Paul VI. The reflection will be based on the reading.

According to God's plan each man is born to promote his own progress since the life of every man is destined by God for some function. From the moment of birth there are implanted the seeds of aptitudes and qualities which are to be developed so that they can bear fruit; their full maturity, however, which man achieves either by education in his own social environment or through his own effort, will cause each person to strive for the end established for him by his Creator. Endowed with intellect and free will, man bears the responsibility both for his own development and for his salvation. Though helped, and at times also impeded, by those who educate him and live in his environment, each individual, whatever influence external circumstances have upon him, is the chief architect of his own fortune good or bad, and merely by exerting the powers of his intellect and will every man can grow in humanity, enhance his value, and perfect himself.

This perfecting of human potentialities is not left to man's good pleasure. As all created things are oriented to their Creator, so creatures endowed with reason are obligated to direct his life by his own will to God as the first truth and highest good. Wherefore this perfecting of the human person is to be considered a summary so to speak of our obligations. Added to this is the fact that the noble harmony of this human nature, which each one by his own effort and the awareness of his duty brings to ever greater perfection, is destined for a higher dignity. Ingrafted in Christ, the giver of life, man receives a new dimension of life and attains to a humanism as it is called which transcends his nature and confers on him the greatest fullness of life to which the perfecting of man looks as to its final goal.[1]

Reflection
- What does our human vocation consist of?
- How can we be more human every day?
- How does our relationship with God and with other people influence our human development?
- Why is personal development of vital importance in God's plan?

Called to live the Gospel

According to the texts we analyzed today, to what kind of communitarian action does becoming aware of our human vocation lead us?

Celebration of our faith:
We share like brothers and sisters

Preparation. Bring a large loaf of bread and background music.

1. The facilitator places the bread on a table and explains the process for the prayer. Then she or he plays some background music and invites everyone to sit around the table in a spirit of meditation and prayer.

2. The facilitator asks a participant to read aloud Matthew 15:29–39.

3. The facilitator invites everyone to meditate on the following aspects of life, leaving a period of silence between each bulleted passage:

- Let us think about the needs for love and belonging in our family, in our small community, and among our friends. What have we done to help meet these needs?
- Let us think about some concrete ways we have made an effort to satisfy our personal growth needs.
- Let us think about people with whom we live who need our love. How do we express our love toward them?
- Let us think about a person we know who has a strong need and ask Jesus, "In what concrete way do you want me to help?" . . . Let us ask Jesus to give us the strength to help.

4. Ask a person from the community to begin by taking a small piece from the loaf of bread and then passing the loaf to the next person. Continue this sharing of the bread until everyone has had the opportunity to take a small piece.

Meanwhile another person guides the community in prayer. After each petition the community responds, "Give us our daily bread."

The shared bread represents all the types of hunger from which we are saved. At the end of the prayer, as an expression of their own union as a community, everyone eats their piece of bread.

- Let us pray for those who are hungry and for those who lack security in their home, their job, or their neighborhood.
- Let us pray for young people who run away from home, for those who drop out of school, and for those who cannot find work.
- Let us pray for young people who are lonely and search for acceptance in gangs.
- Let us pray for those who look for an escape in drugs.
- Let us pray for the children, young people, and adults who are hungry for a life of dignity, who want to be understood and valued by others and by themselves.
- Let us pray for all the people who are hungry for Jesus and who are looking to grow in the love of God.
- The participants are invited to make their own petitions.

5. As we reflect on this community meeting, take some time to listen to what God wants to tell each one of us. Write in your book or diary some phrases that remind you of what God has shared with you today.

6. Invite the community to participate in the following prayer:

Jesus, you who fed five thousand people, help us to be generous with those who suffer from hunger. We praise you right now and worship your presence. We have shared the bread to celebrate our unity in faith and to show our willingness to nourish one another. Help us to be your disciples in our daily life. Amen.

7. Sing a song that speaks about Christian love among people.

COMMUNITY MEETING

Christian Spirituality and Our Image of God

4

For all who are led by the Spirit of God are children of God. For you did not receive a spirit of slavery to fall back into fear, but you have received a spirit of adoption. When we cry "Abba! Father!" it is that very Spirit bearing witness with our spirit that we are children of God.

—Romans 8:14–16

Overview

Objectives

- To discover the images of God that we each hold, in order to prepare to reflect on the meaning of prayer
- To discover the image of God that Jesus shows us

Plan for the meeting

Opening reflection and prayer

Illumination for a Christian spirituality
Commentary 1: Expectations and feelings toward God
Commentary 2: The image of God revealed in Jesus

Celebration of our faith: Growing in faith

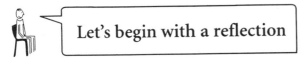

Let's begin with a reflection

In the three previous meetings, we reflected on various aspects of life in light of our relationship as sons and daughters of God, and as brothers and sisters to one another. Today we will examine the image we have of God.

This meeting has a different format and focus than the previous meetings. It is the first meeting dedicated specifically to developing a Christian spirituality. We will begin the meeting with a personal reflection in silence.

Personal reflection
- Draw on a piece of paper your own image of God. Think about the way you see God when you pray and talk to God. This image may be a symbol, like a tree or the sun. Feel free to use abstract imagery if it better captures the way you perceive God.
- Now draw yourself in a way that expresses the type of relationship you have with God.

Prayer based on biblical texts

1. When praying with the following texts, reflect on these two questions:
- How is God revealed in this text?
- What is God telling you, personally, through this text?

2. While you read each scriptural passage, underline or write down one or two words that capture the image of God revealed in it and the message God is communicating to you.

"Is there anyone among you who, if your child asks for bread, will give a stone? Or if the child asks for fish, will give a snake? If you then, who are evil, know how to give good gifts to your children, how much more will your Father in heaven give good things to those who ask him!" (Matthew 7:9–11)

"But if God so clothes the grass of the field, which is alive today and tomorrow is thrown into the oven, will he not much more clothe you—you of little faith?" (Matthew 6:30)

"But I say to you, Love your enemies and pray for those who persecute you, so that you may be children of your Father in heaven; for he makes his sun rise on the evil and on the good, and sends rain on the righteous and on the unrighteous." (Matthew 5:44–45)

For God so loved the world that he gave his only Son, so that everyone who believes in him may not perish but may have eternal life. (John 3:16)

"Then the king will say to those at his right hand, '"Come, you that are blessed by my Father, inherit the kingdom prepared for you from the foundation of the world; for I was hungry and you gave me food, I was thirsty and you gave me something to drink, I was a stranger and you welcomed me, I was naked and you gave me clothing, I was sick and you took care of me, I was in prison and you visited me."'" (Matthew 25:34–36)

"So [the prodigal son] set off and went to his father. But while he was still far off, his father saw him and was filled with compassion; he ran and put his arms around him and kissed him." (Luke 15:20)

"Do not judge, and you will not be judged; do not condemn, and you will not be condemned. Forgive, and you will be forgiven." (Luke 6:37)

Can a women forget her nursing child,
    or show no compassion for the child of her womb?
Even these may forget,
    yet I will not forget you.

(Isaiah 49:15)

3. Read the words you underlined or wrote down and let yourself feel the impact of the images of God and the messages received through the prayer.
• What image of God means the most to you?
• To what type of relationship is God inviting you?

4. Redraw your image of God and your relationship with God. You can keep your original image and add elements to it; you can correct it or alter it slightly; or you can draw an entirely different image. Feel free to reflect on your new perception of, and relationship with, God.

Small-group reflection
In groups of three or four, use the following questions to share your personal prayer experience:
• What did you learn about yourself through your prayer and the reflective exercise?
• What did you learn about God?
• What did you learn about the way you see God?
• What did you learn about the way you relate with God?

Illumination for a Christian spirituality

Our prayer has revealed to us a God who is understanding, kind, generous, life-giving, compassionate, and liberating. The commentaries that follow will allow us to explore more deeply the images and expectations we each have of God. They will help us remember the image of God held by Jesus, which is an image that can accompany us every time we want to pray to God.

Commentary 1: Expectations and feelings toward God

What do we expect of God? Whether we have thought of it or not, we all have expectations of everyone to whom we relate. For example, if a young woman receives a negative reaction from her mother when she admits to a wrongdoing, she will be hesitant to talk about problems with her mother in the future, expecting the same reaction. On the other hand, when a young man is complimented by a teacher for the efforts he has made in writing a paper, he will be encouraged to continue trying, expecting the same type of support the next time.

Building up expectations, be they true ones or false ones, is part and parcel of our humanity. If we are interested in conversing with God through prayer, we should ask ourselves: What do we expect of God?

Let us think for a moment of the ancient Greek and Roman images of gods, which reveal the expectations they had of their deities. Male deities, like Zeus and Vulcan, granted favors and meted out punishments to human beings for particular actions, but they also acted arbitrarily, lost control of their temper, and were lustful. Among the female deities, Venus personified the mystery of love and brought good fortune and victory to her devotees; and Gaea, the earth goddess and mother, the nurturer of all things, personified the natural order.

Among the pre-Hispanic gods were deities represented by animals, like Quetzalcoatl, the feathered serpent, who for the Aztecs was the god of civilization and had attributes both of the bird that flies and the serpent who is powerful and frightening.

In the United States, we use the eye in the triangle to depict God on some of our currency. This image reflects the belief that God is an all-seeing and all-knowing deity who watches over all things.

The Old Testament can reveal a lot to us about God, but we must also remember that the writers of the Old Testament often use a punishing image of God to fight idolatry, injustice, and abuse. For example, Psalm 7 says:

God is my shield,
who saves the upright in heart.
God is a righteous judge,
and a God who has indignation every day.

If one does not repent, God will whet his sword;
he has bent and strung his bow;
he has prepared his deadly weapons,
making his arrows fiery shafts.

(10–13)

Then the psalmist, putting words in King David's mouth, says, "Contend, O Lord, with those who contend with me; / fight against those who fight against me!" (Psalm 35:1).

In the Book of Exodus, we find passages like this one: "I the LORD your God am a jealous God, punishing children for the iniquity of parents, to the third and the fourth generation of those who reject me" (Exodus 20:5).

The New Testament also has vengeful, punishing language, as shown in the following text:

"If any of you put a stumbling block before one of these little ones who believe in me, it would be better for you if a great millstone were fastened around your neck and you were drowned in the depth of the sea. Woe to the world because of stumbling blocks! Occasions for stumbling are bound to come, but woe to the one by whom the stumbling block comes!

"If your hand or your foot causes you to stumble, cut it off and throw it away; it is better for you to enter life maimed or lame than to have two hands or two feet and to be thrown into the eternal fire. And if your eye causes you to stumble, tear it out and throw it away; it is better for you to enter life with one eye than to have two eyes and to be thrown into the hell of fire." (Matthew 18:6–9)

It is important to understand that the writers of both the Old and the New Testaments are persons who, like us, use whatever means they can to try to reform rather intractable human beings. For example, sometimes we hear a parent say to a child, "Listen, if you don't do what I tell you, I'll never take you for a ride again." And we hear a wife tell a husband, "I'll never speak to you again." This is hyperbolic (exaggerated) language, meant to make an impression on the other person and to emphasize the importance of what is being said. Usually it is not intended to be taken literally.

Other negative images of God have come to us through theological reasoning. From the thirteenth century to the early twentieth century, Saint Anselm's theory was a common theory about redemption. According to this theory, although the Son of God had to become human and die a bloody death to make up for the offenses that humans have committed, on their own humans could never reconcile themselves to God because their dignity was infinitely below God's.

The human side of Jesus was identified with those who had offended God, and his divine side was considered to be of the same nature and dignity as God's. Jesus, therefore, could repair the relationship broken by human sin. No significant questions were raised about Saint Anselm's theory until our own century, when people started to ask: What kind of God would require the spilling of blood in order to grant forgiveness and then require *us* to forgive even our enemies by turning the other cheek? Is this the God and Father of Jesus Christ?

Reflection
- What aspects of this commentary helped you to have a better understanding of the origin of the image you have of God?
- What new questions about God came to you from this commentary?

Commentary 2: The image of God revealed in Jesus

It is difficult to relate to God when we have a negative image of God, awakening in us feelings of fear. Fear is an impediment to prayer. To get to know God better, we must get closer by nurturing in our mind and our heart the same image Jesus had of his Father. Otherwise, prayer will continue to be difficult.

From Jesus we learn that God is a loving God who is generous, compassionate, and forgiving. In Jesus' God, there is no vengefulness, no punishment of children from generation to generation for the sins of their parents, no demand of blood in exchange for forgiveness or to provide for the needs of the people. Jesus does not confuse the shortcomings of human beings—our anger, our vengefulness, our hard-heartedness, our desire to inflict punishment—with God's nature and God's way of interacting with us.

The biblical passages we used for prayer earlier reveal some aspects of God's personality. Now we are going to read other passages, paying special attention to how some of God's qualities are manifested. This exercise can be done by following these steps with each of the three sections below:

- One person reads aloud the section.
- The community focuses on how the biblical passages reveal the characteristic of God's personality given in the title of that section.
- One or two community members share about a moment in their life when they have experienced this characteristic of God.

God's generosity. Generosity consists of generating life in others through the sharing of human qualities and spiritual gifts that God has given us, as well as by sharing our time, effort, and material possessions. Jesus understood God's unconditional generosity toward *all* people, lived this same type of generosity, and encouraged his disciples to do the same.
Read Matthew 5:44–45; 6:30; and 7:9–11.

God's compassion. Compassion is a feeling of tenderness and sorrow for the misfortunes of others, along with a desire to alleviate the distress. God feels our sufferings and pains. God's compassion and generosity led to God's incarnation in order to offer us a new life. Jesus continuously shared God's compassion and made it clear to his disciples that God blesses those who are compassionate toward their brothers and sisters with eternal life in the Reign of God.

Read John 3:16; Matthew 25:34–36; and Luke 15:20.

God's merciful love. The story of the prodigal son and the father who receives him back into his house shows us the way God acts (Luke 15:11–32). The father receives with a hug, kisses, and great joy the son who squandered his inheritance. Not only does the father not punish the son or show resentment for what his son has done, he instead organizes a celebration in his son's honor.

When Jesus shows us how to attain God's forgiveness, he describes a simple path that can be followed by anyone willing to overcome pride. He tells us: "'Do not judge, and you will not be judged; do not condemn, and you will not be condemned. Forgive, and you will be forgiven'" (Luke 6:37).

Each and every one of us can expect God to love us unconditionally. God does not love the world in general, God loves each person individually, with a limitless love that does not have any conditions. It means that God does not withdraw love for *any* reason.

Once we come to know the God of Jesus Christ, we can go back to the Old Testament and locate those passages that point to this image of God. God calls the ancient Hebrew people "Israel" in memory of an individual whom God loved very much: Jacob, also called Israel. In certain ways "Israel" thus stands for all of us. The words of the prophet Isaiah to the people of Israel are the same words God speaks to each one of us as members of his new people, the followers of Christ.

Read Isaiah 43:1–4; 49:15–16; and 54:10.

Celebration of our faith: Growing in faith

Preparation. The facilitator must prepare in advance in order to learn the following corporeal prayer:

> Put your arms at your sides and move them up away from the body in a wide circle that ends with hands together above the head. Then bring your hands down in front of your face, pause over your heart, and bring your arms back down to your sides. Repeat this three times, praying silently with the body.

1. Begin this celebration with a personal reflection. In this exercise try to remember the image of God you have carried with you throughout your life. Place a special emphasis on the expectations you have had of God's behavior toward you and on your feelings toward God at each stage of your life. For example, it may be that when you were very young, your image of God was of one who sent an angel to protect you and make you feel safe. Later you might have imagined a God who was giving but regulating, a God who granted you favors in return for your obedience to certain rules. Maybe, at a certain stage, you had an image of a God who inspired fear, or of a judging God ready to condemn you any time you misbehaved.

In order to aid your memory, fill in the chart presented on the following page.

2. The facilitator invites the community to form a circle, to breathe in and out deeply, and to observe a minute of silence in order to enter into a spirit of reflection. Then he or she starts the prayer.

- Lead the corporeal prayer again three times.
- Ask someone to intone the Lord's Prayer for all to sing together, and invite the participants to open their hands, palms up, in front of their body in a spirit of openness and receptivity to God's presence. At the end of the prayer, as the amen is being said, tell the participants to bring their hands across their chest.

3. Everyone sits in the circle, and those who wish to do so, share how they have viewed God over the course of their life and how they view God today. This is done until everyone who wants to do so has had a chance to share their experience.

Stage	Expectations Related to God	Feelings Toward God
Early Childhood (before age 6)		
Childhood (between ages 6 and 12)		
Adolescence (between ages 13 and 15)		
Juventud (over age 16)		

4. Everyone stands up again and repeats the corporeal prayer. At the end the facilitator gives this blessing to her or his peers:

May the God of peace himself sanctify you entirely; and may your spirit and soul and body be kept sound and blameless at the coming of our Lord Jesus Christ. The one who calls you is faithful, and he will do this. (1 Thessalonians 5:23–24)

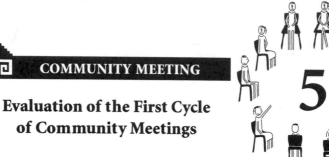

COMMUNITY MEETING

Evaluation of the First Cycle of Community Meetings

Make me know your ways, Yahweh;
teach me your paths.
Lead me in your truth, and teach me,
for you are the God of my salvation;
for you I wait all day long.

Be mindful of your mercy, Yahweh,
and of your steadfast love, for they have been from of old.
Remember not the sins of my youth, or my transgressions;
according to your steadfast love remember me,
because of your goodness, Yahweh!

—Psalm 25:4–7

Overview

Objectives

- To evaluate the first cycle of community meetings
- To celebrate the culmination of the first cycle of community meetings with a prayer and a special gathering or outing

Plan for the meeting

Opening prayer

Conducting and analyzing the evaluation

Celebration of the culmination of the first cycle of community meetings

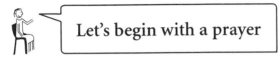

Let's begin with a prayer

The purpose of today's meeting is to evaluate the previous four community meetings. We will start with a prayer on our experience in this cycle of community meetings.

1. Read aloud the epigraph for this meeting to capture its general meaning.

2. Ask each person to reflect briefly on the four community meetings and to think about the impact they have had on his or her life. Afterward invite each person to read the epigraph in silence and choose a phrase that best relates to his or her experience.

3. The person who is facilitating the prayer recites the first sentence: "Make me know your ways, Yahweh; teach me your paths." The people who chose phrases from this sentence pray aloud by responding: "We trust in you and we worship you. Give us your grace, our God." Then the facilitator recites the second sentence, and the people who chose phrases from it, do their prayer aloud. The prayer continues until people who chose from the fourth sentence have prayed aloud.

Conducting and analyzing the evaluation

Evaluation is an indispensable step in the pastoral praxis circle. Evaluating each cycle of community meetings allows the community to examine the quality of the meetings and find ways to improve the Christian praxis of the community. To grow as a community, it is necessary to recognize the successes of living as a Christian community as well as to identify the areas that need further work.

1. Conduct the written evaluation using form 2 in appendix 1, "Evaluation Forms," on pages 182–183. This form has three sections. The first section serves as a general evaluation of the content and process of each community meeting. The content consists of the formation and information elements given in the commentaries, the group activities, and the reflection exercises. The process consists of the methodology, organization, and techniques used to fulfill the objectives of each community meeting. The second section of the evaluation form evaluates community life efforts; the third part helps to identify the fruits that were reaped during this phase, and the areas that still need to be worked on.

Each person should fill out the form according to her or his own experience. Later the community members will have the opportunity to share their opinions.

2. Discuss the written evaluation, based on the instructions given in the "Introduction: Community Meetings," pages 32–33.

3. Summarize the dialog about the evaluation, and record the most significant comments on the community's accomplishments and on the areas requiring more work.

4. After the meeting, analyze the written evaluation by computing the average of each aspect that was evaluated and by making a list of the most significant contributions and recommendations.

5. It is important for the community to file these summaries and compare them to the evaluation of the second cycle of community meetings. The comparison of the evaluations is vital for the community to realize how it is progressing in its faith life, its communitarian organization, and its Christian commitment.

The evaluations also serve as notes on the history of the small community and its growth process. These notes foster a unique sense of identity in the community and may be useful for sharing the community's experiences with new members.

Celebration of the culmination
of the first cycle of community meetings

Have a special gathering or an outing.

FORMATION WORKSHOP

Introduction to Bible Study

"'Do you understand what you are reading?'" [The eunuch] replied, "'How can I, unless someone guides me?'"
—Acts of the Apostles 8:30–31

Overview

Objectives

- To discover that God is present to individuals and to whole peoples through their personal and collective histories
- To learn to study the Bible and become familiar with its principal literary styles

Program

Preparation. Registration, welcome, singing, refreshments, warm-up activity, and initial prayer (1 hour)

Session 1: God is revealed in history (1 hour)

Session 2: How to find books and passages in the Bible (45 minutes)

Session 3: How to identify literary styles in biblical texts (1 hour)

Session 4: God's progressive revelation (1 hour)

Session 5: The Bible, Tradition, and the Magisterium (1 hour)

Session 6: Liturgy of the word (1 hour, 15 minutes)
A. Preparation
B. Celebration

Session 7: Evaluation (45 minutes)

Preparation

When preparing for the workshop, review the section on the formation workshop in the introduction on pages 11–12, and read the instructions on how to prepare the initial journey. Decide if you want to invite people from other types of ministry among youth and young adults, or who are interested in learning about the Scriptures.

While preparations for the workshop draw heavily on the community members' experiences in preparing the initial journey, the workshop itself should be led by a person trained in teaching the Scriptures. The workshop leader should be hired several months ahead of time, so that she or he sets aside the time necessary to prepare and lead the workshop. The workshop leader should be given a copy of this book to help in her or his preparations.

It is crucial that this workshop be consistent with the process of evangelization and formation being experienced in the small communities. The person giving the workshop should employ a participative method that encourages the participants to learn about the Scriptures through group activities and practical exercises. The workshop also offers opportunities for the participants to reflect on what they are learning so that they can internalize the knowledge they are acquiring. The outline of each session offers some directions to help the person giving the workshop fit its content, spirit, and methodology into the overall formation process of the participants.

Note. It is recommended that the participants read the document of the Pontifical Biblical Commission *The Interpretation of the Bible in the Church* (Washington DC: United States Catholic Conference, 1993).

Session 1: God is revealed in history

This session provides a general overview of God's revelation, focusing especially on the following features:
- the geographical and historical context of the events recounted in the sacred Scriptures

- what revelation is and how it occurs within the history of peoples and individuals
- the differences between the revelation in the Old Testament, in Jesus Christ, and in the history of the church

Given the focus on evangelization and formation-in-action in the Prophets of Hope model, it is recommended that you emphasize the following points:

- Revelation is God's communication with humans, making the Divine present in their life to make known God's love and establish with them a relationship of love.
- The sacred Scriptures are the telling of the history of the Covenant that God established with people, and the history of the people who discovered the God of love, mercy, and salvation within their personal and collective histories.
- The revelation of God through words and actions is reflected in our interior life, through other persons, and in the order of the universe.
- It is necessary to have faith—a divine gift—if one wishes to understand how God is revealed and how to respond to God.
- Faith and spiritual life are founded upon the mystery of God, which we can approach in various ways, but which will always remain a mystery.
- God's pedagogy can prepare people for God's explicit and complete revelation in Jesus Christ.

Document 1, "How and Why the Bible Was Written," on pages 162–169, can be used as a resource or as a homework assignment for the participants.

Session 2:
How to find books and passages in the Bible

The objective of this session is for the participants to gain some general knowledge of the books of the Bible, how they are abbreviated, how biblical references are written, and how to find books and passages. Practical exercises are recommended, using citations that trace various aspects of the Covenant. These exercises can be done in small groups, with those who already know how to use the Bible helping those who do not. If all the participants in the workshop know how to do this, the session can be omitted.

Session 3:
How to identify literary styles in biblical texts

The objective of this session is for the participants to discover that the Bible is composed of many diverse **literary genres,** and, through practical exercises, for them to learn to recognize the most important genres. Document 2, "Biblical Literary Interpretation," on pages 170–173, can serve as a guide for the session or as homework for the participants.

Dividing the session into the following three parts is recommended:
- identification by the participants of literary styles common today
- presentation by the workshop leader of the literary styles most relevant in the Bible
- a practical exercise in which workshop participants identify the literary styles of some previously selected passages

Session 4: God's progressive revelation

This session's objective is to demonstrate God's progressive self-revelation in the Old Testament as a preparation for the coming of Jesus, and to emphasize that our knowledge of God is also progressive. It is recommended that you design a reflection exercise in which the participants speak of God's progressive revelation in their life.

Session 5: The Bible, Tradition, and the Magisterium

This session seeks to help the participants understand the relationship between the Bible, the Tradition of the church, and the Magisterium. We recommend making a presentation and then having a question-and-answer session. Document 3, "The Bible and Our Catholic Tradition," on pages 174–179, can be used as a guide or as a homework assignment.

Session 6: Liturgy of the word

Below we offer a framework for helping the participants prepare a liturgy based on their experiences in the workshop. This encourages them to review prayerfully the exercises they did during the day, and allows them to learn how to plan a liturgy.

A. Preparation

The preparation should begin an hour and a half before the liturgy is to take place. The liturgy should draw on the experiences of the day. The following teams will be needed, each with a coordinator.

Altar team. The altar team takes responsibility for arranging a center of focus for prayer, striving to capture the spirit of the day.

Song team. Everyone on the song team receives a songbook, from which they will choose two songs: one for initiating the celebration and one for the ritual of commitment. The team members should practice the songs and be ready to lead the group in singing.

Readings team. It is recommended that the workshop leader give the readings team three readings—one from Genesis or Exodus, a psalm, and one from the Gospels. Three participants are selected to do the readings and are asked to practice them ahead of time in front of the whole team. The others give feedback and suggestions for how to improve the reading presentations.

Reflection team. The reflection is prepared as follows: *(a)* All the members of the team share the most powerful message for strengthening their faith that they heard; *(b)* by consensus they identify the three messages that seem most meaningful for the whole community; *(c)* the participants who shared these three messages prepare to share them with the whole community, speaking for about three minutes each. The other members of the team give suggestions for improving these presentations; *(d)* the workshop leader is asked to be prepared to draw together the reflections of the participants as a conclusion to the reflection.

Offertory team. The offertory team takes charge of choosing some symbols that represent the gifts received during the day, which will be offered to God with prayers for the continued fulfillment of the community and its members. The team assigns members to carry the symbols forward in the offertory procession and present them to God.

Prayers of the faithful team. The prayers of the faithful team decides on five prayers that the group will use to give thanks to God or to ask for light, strength, or forgiveness. The team decides how the participants will respond to these prayers and who will lead the prayers.

Ritual of commitment team. The ritual of commitment team thinks of a simple ritual, with some meaningful symbol, through which all will express their commitment to continue to deepen their knowledge of God's word.

B. Celebration

The following framework below offers a guide to the liturgy:
- Opening song
- Readings: a passage from Genesis or Exodus, a psalm, and a Gospel passage
- Reflection
- Offertory
- Prayers of the faithful
- Ritual of commitment

Session 7: Evaluation

The written evaluation can be done using form 3 found in appendix 1, "Evaluation Forms," on pages 184–185. This form may be photocopied and duplicated. Give the participants twenty minutes to fill out the evaluation. Then facilitate a twenty-five minute session in which the participants share their responses.

COMMUNITY MEETING

A Calling and a Way

Now the Lord said to Abram, "Go from your country and your kindred and your father's house to the land that I will show you."

—Genesis 12:1

Overview

Objectives

- To discover God's calling in our personal history
- To discover that God gives us strength to live out our vocation, and that God gives us the opportunity to rectify our path when needed
- To feel the joy of being part of the long history of faith

Plan for the meeting

Opening prayer

Life experience: The tree of our faith

Illumination leading to action
Commentary 1: Abraham, pilgrim in history and in the faith
Commentary 2: Isaac, the child of the Promise
Commentary 3: Faith and hope in situations of adversity

Celebration of our faith: We offer you our life

Note. Given the richness provided, and the depth of reflection offered by these three commentaries, it is recommended that this theme be the focus of two meetings.

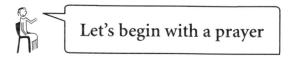

Let's begin with a prayer

We are beginning a series of meetings focused on key aspects of the history of salvation. Let us ask God to help us in our life pilgrimage by praying together:

> God of our life, when we call out to you, you respond.
> You are our guide and our sustenance in our life.
> Have compassion toward us, strengthen our faith,
> and make clear our confusion and doubt.
>
> Lead us in our journey toward you.
> Let us learn good things from those who love us,
> and let us overcome the negative influences
> of hate, violence, and inequity.
>
> Make your marvelous works shine among us,
> and hear us as we invoke your name.
> You give us the confidence
> to continue forward as your community.
>
> Blessed be the Lord!
> Walk with us always,
> and help us to show your way to others
> who seek but do not find you. Amen.

Life experience: The tree of our faith

1. Draw a tree symbolizing the growth of your personal faith. Incorporate the following ideas: *(a)* God is the trunk of the tree; *(b)* we are the fruit of a faith tradition; *(c)* the person who most directly transmitted the faith to us is the branch from which we grow; *(d)* the person who passed the faith on to that person is the branch from which he or she grows, and so on until you go as far back as you can; *(e)* other members of our community or our family who have influenced our faith are the nearby branches; and *(f)* the rest of the church is the other branches.

2. Form small groups of three to four people. Ask the participants to think of a person shown on their tree of faith who has strongly influenced their life. Invite each community member to choose one aspect of this person or a story about her or his religious life to share with the small group.

3. If there is enough time, have each small group choose one of their stories to share with the whole community.

Illumination leading to action

In drawing the tree of our faith, we remembered the people who have transmitted that faith to us, and we spoke of some of their religious experiences. Everyone's faith history develops like this. Today we will reflect on the life of Abraham and how his faith has been passed from generation to generation through the religious experiences of God's people, and through the efforts of the believers to transmit the faith to new people.

Commentary 1: Abraham, pilgrim in history and in the faith

Abraham's story is a religious history.* God called him, and he responded with faith and hope. This faith made Abraham and his wife,

---

*In the culture of Israel, a person's name was linked to their mission. The changing of a person's name meant that God gave them a new mission due to their close relationship with God. For example, *Abram,* which means "exalted ancestor," is later changed to *Abraham,* meaning "ancestor of a multitude." *Sarai,* which means "princess," is later changed to *Sarah,* "mother of kings."

Sarah, break away from their past and take a new road in life, guided by God and confident in God's word. The people of Israel considered Abraham their father in the faith, the first of the patriarchs. As Christians we consider Abraham to be the father of our faith, and he **prefigures** the promised Messiah.

The story of Abraham is found primarily in chapters 11 to 25 of Genesis. The first five books of the Bible (also called the Pentateuch) emphasize different aspects of the patriarchs' religious experience. The **Yahwist tradition** emphasizes God's promises and blessings, the **Elohist tradition** reiterates the patriarchs' faith in the face of many challenges, and the **Priestly tradition** insists on remembering the Covenant and the importance of **circumcision.** These traditions, parts of which were written ten centuries after the actual events occurred, were retold throughout the years by the "children of Abraham," those who came to recognize him as their "father in the faith," finding inspiration in him during crucial moments of their life as the Chosen People. (See document 1, "How and Why the Bible Was Written," on pages 162–169.)

The biblical story of Abraham is paradoxical, repetitious, has many gaps, and cannot be followed as a coherent story through time and space. When reading it we must look for the aspects of Abraham's faith that helped the Israelites to live out their faith and their Covenant with God during particular historical situations.

The people of Israel saw renewed in Abraham the Covenant that God made with our first parents, Adam and Eve. Abraham is such a central figure in the Christian faith that the New Testament mentions him seventy-five times—almost as often as Moses, who is mentioned eighty times. Paul summarizes how the early Christians saw Abraham in his Letter to the Galatians.

Read Galatians 3:26–29.

Throughout history, millions of people have found inspiration in Abraham, especially during times of migration, contact with different religions, and trial to their faith. The story of Abraham shows how God takes the initiative to come to a people at various moments of their history in order to call them to hope for a better life, to bless them and their descendants, to present them a place to have a better life, to give them strength when facing problems, to forgive their failings, and to repay their efforts to remain faithful.

The beginnings of the pilgrimage. Abram and Sarai lived in Ur (an important city in Lower Mesopotamia and a great cultural center of the ancient world) around the year 2000 B.C.E. Abram left Ur with his wife, Sarai, and his nephew, Lot, to settle in Canaan, beginning one of the most significant events of his life: his renouncement of his polytheistic religion in order to trust in a single God. This trust sprang from Abram's deep faith in God, who was revealed to Abram by God's calling Abram forward, showing him a path, and offering him blessings and promises.

Read Genesis 12:1–9.

These promises seemed unlikely to be fulfilled. In addition, for Abram to follow God's call, he would have to abandon his native land, his familiar environment, and his extended family. It would mean changing his lifestyle in order to live with the insecurity of the nomad's constant travels. Abram could not know where he would live or how he would be treated by other peoples and cultures.

It must have been after many struggles and doubts that Abram, Sarai, and Lot set off on the journey. God had promised them that their descendants would make a great nation, but the land in which they arrived was not even theirs. In fact, they remained foreigners in that land even at the time of their death. Furthermore, a large number of descendants seemed impossible: after many years a baby still had not arrived. When, where, and how would these promises be fulfilled?

The journey was long and difficult; Abram, Sarai, and Lot crossed deserts and surely had to confront other tribes and peoples. Finally, after many travels, they arrived in Egypt, fleeing from the hunger that weighed heavily on the lands in which they had sojourned.

Temptation, fall, and mercy. Being chosen by God and responding in faith did not compromise Abram's freedom of choice or his human limitations. Before entering into Egypt, his fear of the future made him succumb to the temptation to abandon his reliance on God and to trust in his own human effort instead. This story prefigures what would happen to Abram's descendants during the Exodus from Egypt.

Read Genesis 12:10–20.

Abram and Sarai's faith was still weak. They placed more trust in their own strategies than in God. This is not to say that they were evil, but they were not holy ones yet, either. Later in Abraham and Sarah's lives, God would continue to bless and sanctify them along their journey of faith.

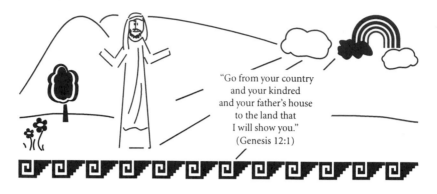

"Go from your country
and your kindred
and your father's house
to the land that
I will show you."
(Genesis 12:1)

Reflection

- Form three groups. One group brainstorms the ways God speaks to youth and young adults; the second group makes a list of what God asks of young people; the third speaks of the promises that God makes to young people who follow God.
- Each of the groups shares its findings with the whole small community.

Called to live the Gospel

Identify the most urgent thing to which God calls your small community today.

Commentary 2: Isaac, the child of the Promise

Chapters 15 to 21 of Genesis tell of Abram's experiences living within God's promise. The following passages allow us to enter into some of those experiences:

- Abram despaired because the child he so urgently desired, the one to whom he would pass on his inheritance, still had not arrived. Yet God again renews this Promise to Abram.
  Read Genesis 15:1–8.
- Abram and Sarai, frustrated that the Promise made to them had not been fulfilled, try to arrange things on their own. Ishmael, son of Abram and Hagar (Sarai's slave) is born.
  Read Genesis 16:1–16.
- God renews the Promise again and makes it clear that Abram will have a child with Sarai, and that the Promise will be fulfilled through that child, Isaac, and not through Ishmael, the son of Hagar.

Read Genesis 17:15–19.

These stories make clear the gracious nature of God's Promise. As Abraham and Sarah aged, it became less and less probable that God's Promise would be fulfilled. Ultimately God rewarded Abraham's willingness to follow the path to which God had called him by blessing him with a son, Isaac.

Reflection

Re-examine God's call to the community that you identified at the end of the previous commentary, and discuss the temptations and problems that could interfere with the community's response to that call.

Called to live the Gospel

What do you need to do to overcome the temptations and problems faced by the community?

Commentary 3: Faith and hope in situations of adversity

Can you imagine how joyous Abram and Sarai must have been when, after so many years of waiting, their son, Isaac, was born? Everything went along well, Isaac was growing up, and his parents were surely already beginning to dream of becoming grandparents. For God had said to Abram, "'Look toward heaven and count the stars, if you are able to count them. . . . So shall your descendants be'" (Genesis 15:5). Yes, Isaac was the first star among a multitude that would one day shine in the immense heavens.

The road to the sacrifice. God sent this elderly couple an awful test. After all these things, God tested Abraham. He said to him, "'Abraham!'" And Abraham replied, "'Here I am.'" God said, "'Take your son, your only son Isaac, whom you love, and go to the land of Moriah, and offer him there as a burnt offering on one of the mountains that I shall show you'" (Genesis 22:1–2). These words choked the heart of the patriarch. How could he give up his son—the one thing he most wanted in life? How could God promise that his descendants would be more numerous than the stars, if his son did not live? Where would he find the strength to sacrifice his own son, Isaac?

Doubts, questions, pain, and confusion assailed Abraham. The God who at first had demanded that they break with their past, now asked Abraham and Sarah to sacrifice their future by offering up their son. They had to choose between God and Isaac. It would seem that keeping Isaac would assure a future and hope for their familial line; saying yes to God would mean falling into the abyss of obscurity, pain, death, and the absurd. What would they do? How mysterious is God when God sends us these dark nights!

Abraham chose God over his own child: "So Abraham rose early in the morning, saddled his donkey, and took two of his young men with him, and his son Isaac" (Genesis 22:3). They walked for three days. Each minute, each step, must have been sheer torment for Abraham. As the tragic moment approached, the anguish tore at his heart, but his faith was strong and he continued walking.

Abraham continued the journey. He was almost at the place of sacrifice. "On the third day Abraham looked up and saw the place far away. Then Abraham said to his young men, 'Stay here with the donkey; the boy and I will go over there; we will worship, and then we will come back to you'" (Genesis 22:4–5).

The last steps of the journey were even worse. Abraham climbed the mountain wearily, as the fatigue of the climb and the pain in his heart took away his voice. Time was running out, and hope was disappearing with it. He was alone with his son; everything was silent. He needed to think and pray, and from time to time he gazed sadly at the youthful silhouette of his son. "Isaac said to his father Abraham, 'Father!' And he said, 'Here I am, my son.' Isaac said, 'The fire and the wood are here, but where is the lamb for a burnt offering?' Abraham answered, 'God himself will provide the lamb for a burnt offering, my son'" (Genesis 22:7–8).

Isaac's question must have broken the heart of the traveler. Perhaps the anguish spilled over into tears, but Abraham continued on his path, maintaining his faith in God. His faith was stronger than his fears and anguish in the face of the sacrifice being asked of him.

An altar to hope

When they came to the place that God had shown him, Abraham built an altar there and laid the wood in order. He bound his son Isaac, and laid him on the altar, on top of the wood. Then Abraham reached out his hand and took the knife to kill his son. (Genesis 22:9–10)

Can you imagine the look of terror and horror on Isaac's face, his cries for mercy when looking at the glint of the blade? In addition, what must Abraham have felt? In two seconds there would be no more Promise, no joy, no hope for him; there would no longer be heaven or stars, only the dark night. Everything would be reduced to a stream of blood spilled upon this mountain. But God intervened:

> The angel of the LORD called to him from heaven, and said, "Abraham, Abraham!" And he said "Here I am." He said, "Do not lay your hands on the boy or do anything to him; for now I know that you fear God, since you have not withheld your son, your only son, from me." (Genesis 22:11–12)

Once again, when he least expected it, God surprised Abraham, and that journey of pain and anguish became one of blessing, joy, and hope. He could look again toward the future and dream; he could contemplate the stars and see in them his descendants. The embrace between father and son amid the solitude of the mountain must have been a sublime moment. Abraham and Isaac were not alone; God accompanied them. So God blessed Abraham, saying,

> "By myself I have sworn, says the LORD: Because you have done this, and have not withheld your son, your only son, I will indeed bless you, and I will make your offspring as numerous as the stars of heaven and as the sand that is on the seashore." (Genesis 22:16–17)

This experience clarified several things. With God, nothing is impossible. God always fulfills promises, offers new opportunities, and renews the calling. This family's God is our God. Abraham and Sarah were the first to believe in God, and each of us is one of those stars that God showed to Abraham one night on a mountain.

The message of this story is one of life. In the time of Abraham, the sacrifice of children was common. God intervened, providing a lamb in place of the child for the sacrifice. This lamb prefigures the lamb that the Israelites later used to celebrate their departure from Egypt and to commemorate their salvation from slavery. Isaac prefigures Christ, who offered himself up on the altar of the cross as the only sacrifice pleasing to God. In the future we may all enter the Promised Land—the Reign of God—as we join ourselves to Christ's sacrifice.

"Do not lay your hand on the boy or do anything to him. . . . By your offspring shall all the nations of the earth gain blessings for themselves, because you have obeyed my voice."
(Genesis 22:12–18)

The God of Abraham is the God of life, the God who offers us his Son to give us eternal life. Abraham's faith is the response of every believer who trusts in the Lord's promises and listens to the call. The faith trials we face arise from life itself. In problems, illnesses, and crises, we, as persons of faith, see the hand of God beckoning us to new life, an ever more abundant life. That is what happened to Abraham. It is also what happens to all people of faith over and over again, in different situations throughout their life.

Reflection
- What are the principal messages of this commentary? Write your answer on a sheet of newsprint.
- Remember the content of the whole meeting (or meetings, if you had two meetings on this topic). Write the key points of the reflection on the newsprint, as well as God's call to live the Gospel, which follows.
- Identify some of the sacrifices you need to make in order to follow God's call.

Called to live the Gospel

In what ways can you help one another so that you are capable of offering the sacrifices to God that indicate following God's call?

Celebration of our faith: We offer you our life

Preparation. Bring a basket, some background music, and small pieces of paper of two different colors, enough so that each participant gets one slip of each color.

1. Prepare a small altar, and put a basket on it for the offering. Give each participant two small pieces of paper of different colors. Play background music during the offering and the rite of commitment.

2. The facilitator invites all to enter into a spirit of prayer, then to write on one of the pieces of paper a heartfelt desire they hope for themselves, and, on the other piece of paper, a heartfelt desire they hope for another person or group of persons. Then the facilitator asks the participants to write on each paper the biggest sacrifice they will have to make in order for these desires to be fulfilled. Afterward have the participants fold the pieces of paper and place them in the basket on the altar.

3. Share the following prayer. All respond, "Hear our prayer," to each petition.

God of our life, when we call out to you, you respond.
- Transform the desires of our heart, so that they might reflect always the desires of your heart. We pray to the Lord. . . .
- Bless the efforts and sacrifices we make to walk with you. We pray to the Lord. . . .
- Accept the labors, anguish, and joys of immigrants who, like Abraham and Sarah, seek land, a future, and a home with dignity for their children. We pray to the Lord. . . .
- Correct the confusion of young people so that they might find their path to you. We pray to the Lord. . . .
- Have mercy on the many suffering families who lack housing, work, and good health. Help us to be generous and to know how to help them. We pray to the Lord. . . .

God, creator of all that is good, we give you thanks for the faith that you give us. We ask you to help us listen to your call, continue our journey, and build with you the history of salvation of all humanity. We ask you this through Jesus Christ, our Lord. Amen.

4. Take some time to listen to what God wants to say to you in light of the message of this meeting. Write a few sentences in your book or diary to help you remember these words from God.

5. Meditate in silence on what you have written. Based on this meditation, commit yourself to some specific effort to respond to God's call.

6. Stand up, and say out loud: "Lord, you know what I have committed to do. Help me to carry it out." All respond, "Amen!"

7. Close the celebration with a song that speaks of the community's faith in God, or with an embrace that reminds us that faith passes from one person to another.

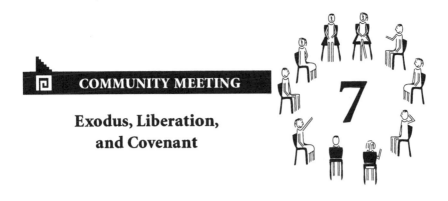

COMMUNITY MEETING

Exodus, Liberation, and Covenant

Then the LORD said, "I have observed the misery of my people who are in Egypt; I have heard their cry on account of their taskmasters. Indeed, I know their sufferings, and I have come down to deliver them from the Egyptians, and to bring them up out of that land to a good and broad land, a land flowing with milk and honey."

—Exodus 3:7–8

Overview

Objectives

- To strengthen our vocation for freedom, as the people of God
- To reflect on the Exodus as a powerful experience of liberation and as the founding event of the Israelite people
- To discover God's call to collaborate in the divine project

Plan for the meeting

Opening prayer

Life experience: Identifying our enslavements and sufferings

Illumination leading to action
Commentary 1: A people lives its history from the perspective of faith
Commentary 2: God's Covenant with people
Commentary 3: Principal lessons of the Exodus

Celebration of our faith: We are part of the people of the Covenant

Note. Given the richness of this theme, we recommend dividing it over two meetings in order to take the time needed to reflect on the biblical readings.

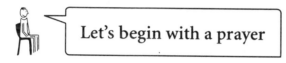

Let's begin with a prayer

The previous meeting focused on the pilgrimage of faith. Today's meeting will focus on faith as a means of liberation from the various kinds of enslavement and suffering that human beings cause as a result of sinfulness. We begin the meeting by asking God to save us from those slaveries that keep us from living according to the plan of love. Each participant can offer a spontaneous prayer asking for a specific kind of liberation. All respond, "Liberate us, Lord."

Life experience:
Identifying our enslavements and sufferings

Preparation. Take to the meeting magazines, newspapers, glue, and any other items appropriate for making a picture collage.

1. Each participant identifies pictures or headlines from magazines or newspapers that illustrate the ways people suffer or are enslaved, choosing examples related to their own experience.

2. Each participant cuts out and glues their pictures or head-lines to one sheet of newsprint or large piece of paper to form one large group collage.

3. All the participants display their collage and explain why they chose the images that they did and how the images are related to their own experiences of enslavement or suffering.

Illumination leading to action

The Israelites suffered many forms of oppression during the period of history when they were exiled in Egypt. In this meeting we will reflect on the way God led them out of Egypt, and on the kind of Covenant made between God and the Israelite people. This reflection will strengthen our faith and help us to face oppression with hope.

Commentary 1:
A people lives its history from the perspective of faith

The descendants of Abraham, Isaac, and Jacob went to Egypt in search of food and well-being, for in the region they had lived, there was a great drought and their livestock were dying of hunger. They asked the authorities in Egypt, a rich and prosperous country, to allow them to remain there. At first they found the pastures and food they needed, but later they were enslaved, and what had been a deliverance into well-being became an experience of injustice, misery, and oppression. Moved by the suffering of the Israelites, God would later call Moses to liberate his people and lead them to the Promised Land.

The exit from Egypt and the journey toward the Promised Land are known as the Exodus, which means "road out." Events of this period in the history of the people of Israel are related in several books of the Old Testament, especially in the Book of Exodus. The crucial experiences of the Exodus occurred under Moses' exceptional leadership. God liberated the Israelites from slavery, formed a Covenant with them, and made them encounter both the sin in their heart and divine mercy. This God remained mysteriously present with the people in order to accompany them in the eternal process of human liberation and salvation from sin.

God prepares Moses to be a prophet of liberation. Many years after the Israelites' arrival in Egypt, fearful of their rapid population growth, Pharaoh decreed that all male Israelite children would be killed at birth. This news horrified the Israelites, but God acted through some of the Egyptian midwives to save the boys. The midwives disobeyed Pharaoh and refused to assassinate the Israelite boys. This was one of the first cases of civil disobedience, in which people obeyed God before obeying the king.

One of the Israelite women gave birth to a male child and kept him hidden for three months. Fearing that he would be killed, the woman left the child in a basket on the waters of the Nile River, in the hope that Pharaoh's daughter would find him, feel tenderness toward the child, and rescue him. This is exactly what happened: Pharaoh's daughter took mercy on the child, saved him from the river, and named him Moses, which means "drawn out of the water." Moses' older sister offered to find a woman to nurse the child, and chose Moses' mother to do so. Thus Moses was raised with the love of his own mother and educated as a prince in Pharaoh's palace.

While Moses grew up, the oppression of the Israelite people increased. They cried out to God and thought that God did not hear them, not knowing that God had already answered their prayers by saving their future liberator from death.

Moses experiences the injustice suffered by people of his race. Rejection by people of his own race and threats from Pharaoh were constants in Moses' life, up until the time that he fulfilled his mission of liberation. The life of other prophets, including Jesus, is marked by the same pattern of rejection and threats, but, in the end, God always aids in the fulfillment of their missions, which sooner or later bear fruit. The Acts of the Apostles retells the story of Moses in order to remind the first Christian communities of their origins.
Read Acts of the Apostles 7:24–28.

Moses encounters God. Moses thought that he would live out his life as a shepherd in the desert. But God had other plans.
Read Exodus 3:1–15.

In chapter 3 of Exodus, God appears to Moses through a powerful sign: a burning bush, in which the fire burns without consuming. In this encounter God reveals God's name to be Yahweh, which means "'I AM WHO I AM'" (3:14). God also says, "'I AM has sent me to you.'" With this name the people of Israel understood that God was present and active among them.

Yahweh is a God of life who shows himself to be sensitive to injustice. God chooses Moses to be an emissary and spokesperson, a prophet. Moses resists, for he fears failure; he insists to God that no one will believe him, and he protests that he does not have the abilities necessary for this kind of leadership. He asks God to send someone else. But in the face of God's insistence, Moses gives in and agrees to fulfill God's mission.

"Do not be afraid, stand firm,
and see the deliverance
that the LORD will
accomplish for you today."
(Exodus 14:13)

God reveals an opposition to injustice. At the beginning of his mission, Moses stood alone. Pharaoh did not want to liberate the Israelite people because he needed the cheap labor they provided for his construction projects. Even the people themselves did not believe Moses. But with God's help, Moses conscienticized the Israelites about the call of God for their liberation and the need to flee from the injustice.

Finally, after suffering a series of trials and plagues, Pharaoh agreed to let the Israelites go out of the country. He soon regretted having let them go and sent an army to recapture them. However, the Israelite people passed through the Red Sea without difficulty, whereas the Egyptians drowned in its waters. The Israelites recognized in these events "the strong arm of God" who had saved them from slavery in Egypt.

The Bible calls the series of events that happened the night that the Israelites escaped Egypt under the protection of God the

Passover, or the transition from slavery to liberation. From that experience on, Passover meant the great spring in which God liberated them from the Egyptian yoke through a series of providential interventions.

Ancient creed and worship. The escape from Egypt was the Israelites' fundamental experience of God's liberating action, the work of this God of Abraham, Isaac, and Jacob. This faith experience was transmitted from parents to children down through many generations, both orally and through ritual celebrations. Through this process, there developed the oldest creed known regarding the God of this Chosen People, a creed that remained alive through liturgical celebrations held in remembrance of these events.

Read Deuteronomy 26:1–10.

The first thing Moses did after leaving Egypt was to lead the whole of God's People in offering up a sacrifice of adoration and gratitude. Throughout their entire history, the Israelite people have looked back and remembered God's intervention as their liberator. Out of this experience of God, the Israelites made their Covenant with God and reflected on their history as a people of faith.

Reflection

1. Think of an experience related to some form of oppression in which you have felt God's liberating action.

2. Share these experiences of liberation.

Called to live the Gospel

Analyze, in light of your own experience and the reflection above, the experiences of liberation that were shared in the group. Try to identify some actions you can engage in to become a source of liberation for members of the small community, for other young people, and for the wider society.

Commentary 2: God's Covenant with people

In the face of the hunger and thirst that they faced in their escape to the desert, the Israelites were tempted to return to slavery. But God protected them by sending them water and food (manna), thus helping them to remain faithful on the road to freedom. Chapters 16 and

17 of the Book of Exodus tell of the various ways that God showed the Israelites love and care. In this way they were gradually prepared for their first Covenant with God as a *unified people,* no longer as separate tribes and families as in the times of the patriarchs.

The key event of the Exodus is the religious Covenant that God made with the Israelites. Sociopolitical liberation from Egypt was the beginning of something deeper: God would make the Israelites, now free, the Chosen People, a holy nation consecrated to God's service. Through this Covenant, sealed by the Ten Commandments, the Israelites were newly constituted as a people, no longer seeing themselves only as the tribes descended from Israel.

The most important aspect of the Covenant is that God commits to the Chosen People forever, and God asks in return that they demonstrate love for God and show a special respect for other people. The Book of Exodus tells us that during their journey in the desert, the people were unfaithful to God many times. But when they repented of this and reformed their lives, God forgave them and reestablished the Covenant that had been broken by their sin.

Read Exodus 20:1–17.

Reflection

Go over the Ten Commandments of the Covenant. Decide together which two commandments, if kept, would most powerfully and positively influence the life of community members today. Explain why you chose these two commandments.

Called to live the Gospel

- Form groups of four or five people. Discern together what the community can do to help all its members better keep the two commandments chosen above.
- Share your reflections with the whole small community.

Commentary 3: Principal lessons of the Exodus

The Book of Exodus recounts a journey full of stumbling blocks, difficult times, mistakes, and anguish—but a journey guided by hope, guaranteed by faith, and directed by God's love. It is a journey forever renewed, in which new strength ultimately overcomes weariness; the desire for faithfulness to the Covenant overcomes sinfulness; and people gradually realize that God wants them to be free and shows them the road to true happiness. The Book of Exodus contains many teachings for us Christians. Here we note the principal ones:

Our God is a God of justice and liberation. God wants to free people from their enslavements of sin, oppression, and misery, both individual and social. The Book of Exodus shows the passage from sin to grace, from evil to good, from death to life.

Moses prefigures Christ. Moses carried, for the Israelites, the burden of liberation, and became a mediator to gain forgiveness for their personal and social sins; he led the people to the Promised Land. Christ is the liberator of all humanity, the redeemer of each individual, and the savior of all peoples on earth. Christ leads us to the fullness of the Reign of God.

The Passover in Exodus prefigures the Easter mystery. The liberation from slavery in Egypt, passing from a situation of death to one of life, prepares us to understand that through Jesus' death and Resurrection, God made possible victory over evil and eternal life in lov-

ing communion with God. The Passover lamb used to celebrate the departure from Egypt has become for Christians a symbol of Christ, the paschal lamb offered up for the salvation of all humanity.

The Israelites had to cross a desert to arrive in the Promised Land. All liberation, whether it be personal, social, or spiritual, is a long and difficult journey. Liberation requires effort and commitment. As experienced by the Israelite people in the desert at Sinai, the road to liberation is full of temptations, infidelities, doubts, and yearnings to return to the comfort of what we have always known. But God accompanies us and gives us strength for the journey.

The Covenant of the Exodus prefigures Christ's Covenant with us. The Covenant of the Exodus is usually called the First Covenant. In that event God commits to liberate Israel from Egyptian oppression, to make the Israelites the Chosen People, and to prepare them for the definitive Covenant through worship, the Law, and the prophets. Christians understand this definitive Covenant to have arrived with Jesus, the messiah. This later Covenant is called the New Covenant, or the New Testament; in it we live in Christ and form the new people of God, the Body of Christ. The New Covenant is not only with the Israelite people but with all of humanity.

The Ten Commandments are preparation for the Gospel of Jesus. The Book of Exodus is the book of the Law. In it are found the guidelines for how the Israelite people should live in order to maintain their Covenant with God. Under the New Covenant, fulfilled in Jesus Christ, we must not only fulfill the Ten Commandments, we must also live the Gospel, the new law of Christ.

Reflection
- Read in silence the preceding teachings, and choose the one that carries the most important message for your life.
- Share the teaching that you chose with the whole community, explaining why it is so important for your life.

Called to live the Gospel
Given what everyone shared, to what do you feel called as a community of young people?

Celebration of our faith:
We are part of the people of the Covenant

Preparation. Bring two candles, matches, some sandals, a staff, a bag or pack, a loaf of bread, and a water canteen.

1. Put a Bible on the altar along with the rest of the objects. Explain the process for the celebration.

2. Begin with a song that speaks of journeying and pilgrimage. It should be sung while walking in procession inside the meeting room or, preferably, while entering from the street or hallway.

3. Read Psalm 135.

4. Join in a shared reflection based on the following question: What does the experience of the Exodus tell us about our God, our history as a people of faith, our personal life, and our vocation?

5. Take some time to listen to what God wants to say to you regarding the message of this meeting. Write in your book or diary some reminders of God's words to you.

6. Again, form a procession, this time toward the altar. As the participants arrive at the altar, ask them one by one to choose a displayed symbol that speaks to their heart. Each member holds the chosen symbol, prays aloud if he or she feels comfortable doing so, and then returns the symbol to the altar for the other participants to use. The whole community responds to each prayer by singing, "Lord, hear our prayer."

7. End the meeting with one or two stanzas of the opening song.

Jesus, the New and Eternal Covenant

For

there is one God;
there is also one mediator between God and
humankind,
Christ Jesus, himself human,
who gave himself a ransom for all

—this was attested at the right time.

—1 Timothy 2:5–6

Overview

Objectives

- To reflect on Jesus as the full revelation of God in our history
- To discover that the New and eternal Covenant promised in the Old Testament is fulfilled in Jesus

Plan for the meeting

Opening prayer

Life experience: Persons and significant acts in history

Illumination leading to action
Commentary 1: Jesus becomes incarnated in salvation history
Commentary 2: Jesus' mission to announce the Reign of God
Commentary 3: Jesus lives in history

Celebration of our faith: Witnesses to the Covenant with Jesus

Note. Given the richness of this theme and the depth of reflection necessary to benefit fully from it, we recommend covering this theme over the course of two meetings.

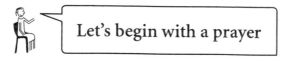

Let's begin with a prayer

This meeting will focus on Jesus as the New and everlasting Covenant. We will start by praying together a litany of names that are applied to Jesus. After each name, all should respond, "Blessed are you, O Lord!"

Jesus, Word of God	Jesus, Lamb of God who takes away sin
Jesus, eternal wisdom	Jesus, king of justice and peace
Jesus, Son of God	Jesus, the Way, the Truth, and the Life
Jesus, Son of Abraham	Jesus, who saves us from our sins
Jesus, Son of Mary	Jesus, image of the invisible God
Jesus, Son of Joseph	Jesus, gentle and humble of heart
Jesus, beloved Son	Jesus, advocate for the needy
Jesus, the Messiah	Jesus, prophet of the Reign
Jesus, the carpenter	Jesus, wonderful counselor
Jesus, Savior of the world	Jesus, Resurrection and life
Jesus, faithful witness	Jesus, New and eternal Covenant
Jesus, good shepherd	Jesus, beginning and end
Jesus, bread of life	Jesus, cornerstone of the church
Jesus, light of the world	Jesus, head of the Body, the church

Life experience:
Persons and significant acts in history

    1. Form two groups. One will come up with a short description of the contributions made by a famous historical figure of its choosing; the other will describe briefly the principles and ideals that led to the formation of the United States or the country of origin of one of the group's members.

    2. Each group shares its description with the community.

    3. In community, everyone tries to identify the impact that the historical figure and the principles and ideals of the country described have had on today's society and on their own life.

Illumination leading to action

History moves forward day by day. A huge number of events go by imperceptibly; others are so significant that they attract attention to themselves. The previous exercise reminded us of two kinds of significant events:

- The actions of persons who have made an impact on history with their ideals and thoughts; with their values, principles, and feelings; with their message; and with their hopes for humanity. When we share and admire these persons and what they value, we make them our models and heroes, and they become part of our life.
- Key moments in the history of a nation become points of reference for fixing its origin, valuing its past, and giving direction to its future: for example, the national constitution, the name of the country, and the ideals of its founders.

    In this meeting we will reflect on Jesus as a person who made a mark in history with the establishment of the New Covenant promised to the people of Israel. We will see how Jesus' life, death, and Resurrection marked the beginning of a new way of living and a new way of understanding history.

Commentary 1: Jesus becomes incarnated in salvation history

Jesus is the center and the protagonist in God's revelation within salvation history. Jesus of Nazareth is the full expression of the always-present dialog between God and humanity, the complete revelation of God to Israel and to all of humanity. In Jesus we find the meaning of our origins and our life.

In the mysteries of Jesus' life, we capture the full meaning of the Covenant that God established with humanity. In the mystery of the Incarnation, the dignity conferred on human beings becomes clear once again. In all this the freedom of each human being is respected; each person has the option to recognize the Son of God or to not recognize him. The stories of Joseph, who accepted the mystery of Jesus; of the shepherds and wise men who went to adore and honor him; and of Herod, who wanted to kill him; show us humanity's options in coming face-to-face with this child who is God.

Jesus became a human like us in everything except sin. This is true not because it was easier for him, as God, to avoid sin. Rather, Jesus remained sinless because, as the most excellent human, sin

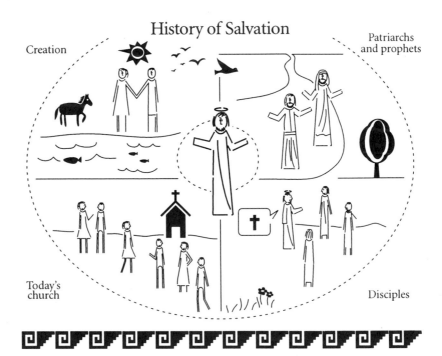

History of Salvation

Creation

Patriarchs and prophets

Today's church

Disciples

(that is, anything that goes against the human person) cannot be a part of him. In recognizing Jesus Christ's humanity, a new hope is born for all people and for each person. Jesus' Incarnation affirms that we are called to holiness, and that we are not slaves to sin. God's plan was always to give life, never to condemn or punish humanity; this was made clear in Jesus. The consequences for sin do not have dominion over Jesus, and sin does not hold dominion over Christians who live out their Covenant with God.

Reflection
Share some ways Jesus has helped you to abandon behaviors that destroy you or that harm other people.

Called to live the Gospel
Identify some ways that members of the community could assist one another to abandon behaviors that hurt themselves or other people.

Commentary 2: Jesus' mission to announce the Reign of God

Jesus began his ministry with his baptism at the Jordan River, where he received the revelation of his filial relationship to God the Father. In this revelation God's solidarity with humanity is once again proclaimed.

Jesus' mission can be summarized as establishing the Reign of God by proclaiming and making present God's love for all people. Jesus made present the Reign in the historic context of his people, announcing it from within his own tradition, making it real within the situation in which he lived. In this way he fulfilled the message of the Commandments and the prophets as Jesus himself said: "'I give you a new commandment, that you love one another. Just as I have loved you, you also should love one another. By this everyone will know that you are my disciples, if you have love for one another'" (John 13:34–35).

Jesus' works, attitudes, and actions among the people, together with his teachings and miracles, are signs of the new life that had been announced by the prophets. It is this same Covenant with God that now is opened clearly to all humanity, a love that is translated into constant concern for all human beings. The Covenant with God did not end with the event at Sinai, but rather is, from the life of

Jesus onward, a Covenant realized in all the followers of Jesus and made concrete when we proclaim and make present the Reign of God through our actions of love, justice, and peace. Five dimensions of this New and eternal Covenant established by Jesus continue to be realized today in our life. These dimensions are as follows:

1. God is community. The mystery of the Incarnation of the Son and God's sending of the Spirit to the Christian community reveal to us the trinitarian mystery of God the Father, God the Son, and God the Holy Spirit: the community of God-love. Jesus calls his disciples to carry the Good News to all peoples of the earth and to form a community, following this model of God-community. In this way Jesus places the foundations of the church as a community of believers and as the **sacrament** of Christ.

We, as persons baptized in Jesus Christ, cannot live in isolation. The spirit of God manifests itself in our communitarian solidarity and in our participation in the Eucharist.

2. God wants life, dignity, and freedom for all persons. The provident God of the Creation continues the living presence among people through Jesus, who receives and forgives sinners; heals the sick, feeds the hungry, frees those enslaved, and honors the humble; identifies himself with the poor, the disenfranchised, and those despised by society; and even gives new life to the dead. Jesus still performs these actions among us and through us, continually revealing himself as the God of life. He continues changing lives that seemingly have no meaning, healing broken hearts, opening new doors and paths, respecting and valuing those cast out from society.

As the community of Jesus, it is our role to make God present among people. This is to say that, like Jesus, we should constantly promote the life, dignity, and freedom of all human persons.

3. God makes a preferential option for the poor. Jesus shows God's option for the poor. He was born into a poor family, in a stable outside the city because there was no place for them in the places travelers usually lodged; the first announcement of his birth was made to shepherds, who were poor; his parents offered two doves for him at the presentation in the Temple because they were poor; the Apostles were humble people, not wise or rich; Jesus' preaching constantly proclaimed God's favor for the poor and the humble of heart. God's strategy is to make known the New Covenant of the Son through the life of the poor.

The arrival of the Reign of God occurs, first of all, among the poor. As followers of Jesus, we, too, must give the poor a privileged place within our heart and in our actions. This preference means seeing life from their perspective whenever their lives, dignity, and freedom are at risk, and it means being in solidarity with their struggles for liberation and justice.

4. The New Covenant is born of love. God stops at nothing to give us life, even sending the Son among us. Jesus' life and message bear clear testimony to this divine love. The promise of land made to Abraham and to the Israelites now extends to the promise of a new heaven and a new earth built on love among persons. Just as the people of Israel prepared themselves to conquer the Promised Land during their sojourn in the desert, we as the people of God must strive to live out our commitment to love.

5. The New Covenant is sealed by the Resurrection of Jesus. The Resurrection is the seal of the New Covenant. Through the Resurrection, this God-made-human defeated death and achieved eternal life for himself and for each of us. Jesus' Resurrection reveals our own future: after death, we will live with him. The Resurrection is the root of our hope and from it springs the possibility of our complete fulfillment. As prophets of hope, our role is to bear witness to our confidence in God's faithfulness and to our faith that we will reach eternal life by fulfilling the commandment of love.

Reflection
Review the dimensions of the Covenant presented above and discuss the following:
- What is the easiest dimension for you to understand and accept? Why?
- What dimensions are the most challenging for each individual and for the community?

Called to live the Gospel
Brainstorm different ways the community members can help one another live out the Covenant with God.

Commentary 3: Jesus lives in history

As we have seen by looking at the lives of famous persons, we know people more through their most significant actions than through the details of their life. In the Gospels we find few specific details about Jesus' life, but the Gospels show his actions. The reflections of the early Christian communities presented to us by the Gospel writers complete the picture.

The paschal mystery: Proof of God's love. Jesus' Passion, death, and Resurrection give us certainty of God's fidelity to the Covenant. To give us life, God does not withhold even God's own Son's life. Jesus' Passion and death show the magnitude of God's identification with humankind, and Jesus' Resurrection shows that death has been defeated. It no longer holds dominion over us. From now on, the meaning of pain, of sacrifice, of illness and death are all tied to life itself: the option for love and life is the only thing that endures.

The new life of the Resurrection, in which we participate by our baptism, is the hope of the disciple who knows that giving one's life for the Gospel gains us everlasting life. The first priority of our life of faith is commitment to love. The offering of our life in service to our neighbors is the measure of our fidelity to the New Covenant.

The church: Sacrament of Jesus. The community of believers recognizes in Jesus the full revelation of God, and it is through that community that we know God and we receive his life. The commitment of the New Covenant is to be the channel of God's grace and to continue the mission given to us by Jesus: to go throughout the world and make disciples of all people—disciples who embrace the commitment of giving their life for their neighbors, as Jesus did.

In Jesus Christ we always find the source of our mission. Jesus' life and praxis are our model. We are called as a church to be the instruments of Jesus, the witnesses who make present his salvific words and actions in our historical moment.

Reflection

1. Think about how Jesus' Resurrection affects our life as a community of baptized persons by reflecting on the following questions:

- How do we live out our experience of being a risen people resurrected with Jesus?
- How do we celebrate the Resurrection through the sacraments?

2. On a large sheet of paper, draw an emblem or insignia that expresses how the community lives out its experience of the risen Jesus.

Called to live the Gospel

In light of this meeting's reflection and the insignia you have just made, identify the areas in which you need to grow in your experience and in your witness to the certainty of Jesus' Resurrection in you and among you.

Celebration of our faith: Witnesses to the Covenant with Jesus

Preparation. Bring a Bible, one large candle, matches, and a small flag for each of the community members. The flags can be made using wooden sticks and note cards, with bases made from modeling clay.

1. Place a small altar on the ground, with a Bible and a lit candle on it. Give each participant a flag.

2. Sing a song that speaks of us as members of the people of God actively building the Reign. Sing one or two verses.

3. Read Mark 16:15–20. Afterward join in a shared reflection based on the following questions:
- What challenges does this mission present to us today?
- What signs indicate that we are making the Reign of God present among people?

4. Take a little time to listen to what God wants to say to you in light of this meeting's message. Write in your book or diary some phrases to remind you of God's words.

5. The facilitator invites the community members to do the following:

- Write down on the flag an action or teaching of Jesus to which you want to bear witness within this community or among your friends or family.
- Think about what kind of conversion is required in order to bear this witness—purifying your feelings? strengthening your will? taking action? gaining more intellectual training? attaining greater abilities in another way?
- Write down the aspects of your personal life that need work, with God's help, in order for you to be a better witness to Jesus.

6. Form a procession, all going forward to deposit your flag on the altar. Place the flags in a circle around the candle and the Bible to symbolize the desire to be a community of witnesses. As each person places his or her flag on the altar, he or she says aloud, "Lord, help me to be your witness." All respond, "Listen to our prayers, we ask as your community."

7. Finish by singing a few more verses of the opening song.

Coprotagonists with God in History

Thus says God, the LORD, . . .
I am the LORD, I have called you in righteousness,
   I have taken you by the hand and kept you;
I have given you as a covenant to the people, . . .
      to open the eyes that are blind,
   to bring out the prisoners from the dungeon
      from the prison those who sit in darkness.

—Isaiah 42:5–7

Overview

Objectives

- To build awareness that history is built through the multiple and diverse experiences that constitute personal life and the life of a people
- To increase social sensitivity to the situation in which Hispanic people live in the United States
- To encourage conscious participation in history as coprotagonists with God

Plan for the meeting

Opening prayer and life experience: A people on a journey

Illumination leading to action
Commentary 1: A migrant people, builders of history
Commentary 2: Builders of salvation history
Commentary 3: Faith, hope, and love as driving forces of history

Celebration of our faith: Building history with God

 Let's begin with a prayer

Since we began reflecting on our Covenant with God, we have gradually become more conscious of our collaboration with God in history. Today we will focus on the invitation to be **coprotagonists** with God in history. Our opening prayer will be combined with our reflection on our life experience.

Opening prayer and life experience: A people on a journey

1. The objective of this exercise is to identify how you or someone you are close to has helped to build history. In silence, choose the person you will focus on and think about how this person has influenced others in a positive way and given direction to her or his own life, the life of her or his family, her or his class or work mates, or a sector of society.

2. Write two phrases on a small piece of paper: one to express the action or actions taken by the person that collaborated in the building of history, the other to express the positive and determinant consequences of the action. Then share what you wrote.

3. Reflect as a community on what it means to build history in the world today.

4. Those who wish to do so may pray over the experiences that were shared. All respond, "Hear our prayer."

Illumination leading to action

During the life experience part of the meeting, we shared some ways we or people we are close to have been builders of history. The following commentaries will help us reflect on how various forces have an impact on the building of history.

Commentary 1: A migrant people, builders of history

Great movements of large populations have occurred many times in history, and these migrations have often been painful. Generally the journey is slow, difficult, and tragic in many ways. Many people die without ever fulfilling their dreams of reaching a place that will give them life and sustenance. Our indigenous ancestors migrated until they found the lands that they made their own, where their cultures developed and where they gave life to succeeding generations. The same thing occurred with the Europeans who arrived in the Americas five centuries ago. All were immigrant peoples.

Recently many people from Latin America, Asia, and Africa have had to emigrate in order to escape poverty or violence in their countries of origin. Many people have chosen to come to the United States.

Every migration is difficult, whether it is made across oceans or through unknown lands. Having to share natural resources with other groups and relate to people who have a different language, culture, or religion is always challenging—for the immigrants as well as for the peoples already established in the places where the immigrants settle. Each people confronts these challenges in various ways, depending on their culture and religion. Oftentimes, the stronger people—those holding the greater resources—end up dominating, marginalizing, exploiting, or annihilating the weaker people.

Immigrants with hope. The history of the Latino people of the United States is made up of generations of immigrants from greatly diverse backgrounds, some established in these lands more than five hundred years ago, others only recently arrived. Thousands of people annually cross the borders into the United States. Their determined faces reflect their desire to move ahead and build better lives, which they find almost impossible in their own countries. For most, leaving their own country tears at their heart. However, they risk all they have on an uncertain future, becoming a people in search of hope and open to the possibility of never returning to their native land.

To migrate is to move from one place to another. Migration is a visible sign of a humble journey in hope of finding a new life. It implies taking risks, giving up established ways, and exploring; it requires a spirit of courage and a willingness to struggle to overcome obstacles. When they emigrate, Hispanic people carry with them deep values of love and sacrifice, along with their language, culture, and the symbols that define their identity. In general, they are a people of faith who leave their home countries with faith in God, in themselves, and in the country to which they journey. This faith and trust in God's protection motivates them to continue their journey until they finally arrive at their destination.

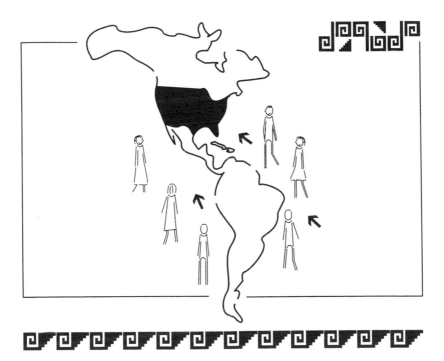

Migrants show their sense of community and solidarity through heroic actions, risking their life or their well-being for others, rescuing those who fall by the wayside or suffer from sickness. A powerful sense of service and compassion exists among them. This finds concrete expression in their efforts to heal the wounds of those injured on the journey; to share blankets, money, or food with those who have none; to console those who mourn; and to encourage those who lose heart. When they arrive at their destination, some immigrants are greeted by the open arms of family members or friends; others encounter a hostile world. The majority do not speak the local language, and they experience cultural and psychological shocks that affect their personal stability, which is often already damaged by the misery or violence from which they fled.

Keeping faith in God and growing in that faith may require extra effort for many immigrants for several reasons: because of the changes and cultural shocks they have experienced, because this is their first encounter with a society of religious pluralism, or because of their sudden insertion into the secularized and materialistic aspects of modern U.S. culture. Immigrant young people, therefore, require a strengthening of their relationship with God through an encounter with Jesus as alive and active within their own history.

Immigrants with serious challenges. The advance of technology, violence, **economic neoliberalism,** and rapid population growth have led to massive mobility among rural sectors in Latin America. Many *campesinos* and indigenous people migrate from rural areas to large cities when they find that their lands can no longer sustain their families, but they then lack the economic means to survive, obtain medical care, live in sanitary conditions, or provide education for their children. The transition from an agricultural-based life to a lifestyle in which education and technology are necessary conditions for survival can bring serious challenges to one's value system and, at times, to one's faith.

Other persons immigrate to the United States in hope of protecting their life, improving their economic situation, or fulfilling a dream. They do not realize the shock they will experience because of the disparity between their roots and their new reality, between a "Third World" society and the "First World," between Latin culture and Anglo culture. Even less do they realize the consequences these clashes will have on their personal life and the life of their family.

The United States does not always receive immigrants with open arms, especially if they belong to disadvantaged sectors of society. Since 1882 the U.S. government has passed various laws to regulate and control the entrance of immigrants into the country. These laws are applied above all to nonwhite people of limited resources. But no law has been able to stop the massive arrival of people in search of a better life.

Many immigrants come to find work without having legal work papers. As a result, they are subject to extortion and exploitation in the jobs they do find, or they have to resort to using false names and documents. The buying and selling of documents and false names exposes many Latinos to the risk of being incarcerated or deported; it affects their sense of identity; and it undermines their freedom to become involved in social groups, including the church. But at times it is their only alternative for finding work. The price is high, but luck or audacity and cleverness allow them to survive and to better their situation.

Reflection
- Ask two or three community members who have immigrated to the United States to share the most difficult challenges they have faced.
- Invite the whole community to identify the greatest challenges that immigrants from various cultures encounter in their local area. Brainstorm a list of ideas, and then pick out the two or three greatest challenges.
- Identify the greatest challenges the community must overcome in order to accept immigrant individuals and groups coming from cultures different from its own.

Called to live the Gospel
In the face of the challenges mentioned above, discuss the following questions:
- What should be our small community's response?
- What do we need to do to make this response a reality?

Commentary 2: Builders of salvation history

God calls us to work to build history. Some of us are called to glorify God in a strange land; others, to embrace the foreigner as a son or daughter of God. All of us, with our diverse origins, customs, and cultures, are called to shape a new society guided by the mind and heart of God.

The Christian faith must always be rooted in the historic situations in which people live. When faith is separated from the history of people, it becomes a dead or an empty faith. Younger generations, therefore, have a vital historical mission, because by living in the present according to God's plan, they give direction to the future through their ideals, values, and life projects.

Immigrants and citizens, together in history. In the Judeo-Christian tradition, the traveler and the foreigner are symbols of human beings who struggle to survive and improve their life. Since the beginning of salvation history, the Israelite people have taught us the necessity of having an attitude of openness and acceptance to strangers, treating them with dignity and respect. Indeed, exploiting or alienating strangers was prohibited: "You shall not oppress a resident alien; you know the heart of an alien, for you were aliens in the land of Egypt" (Exodus 23:9). Ancient Christian philosophy, expressed in the Letter to the Hebrews, ratifies this same sentiment: "Let mutual love continue. Do not neglect to show hospitality to strangers, for by doing that some have entertained angels without knowing it" (13:1–2).

Immigration is a right of all individuals and peoples, and it has been defended officially as such by the Catholic church for generations. But modern society has denigrated the profound human meaning of migration through borders and laws. In the face of this reality, Pope Paul VI, in his apostolic letter *A Call to Action: On the Occasion of the Eightieth Anniversary of the Encyclical "Rerum Novarum" (Octagesima Adveniens),* declares the right to emigrate:

> We are thinking also of the precarious situation of a great number of emigrant workers whose condition as foreigners makes it all the more difficult for them to make any sort of social vindication, in spite of their real participation in the economic effort of the country that receives them. It is urgently necessary for people to go beyond a narrowly nationalist attitude in their regard and to give them a charter which will assure them a right to emigrate, favor their integration, facilitate their professional advancement and give them access to decent housing where, if such is the case, their families can join them.[2]

We forge salvation history in our daily life. Salvation history is tied to daily life, rather than to geography; it is part of the history of individuals and whole peoples, wherever they are found. The people of Israel encountered God in the midst of their history. Both during times of migration and times of greater stability, God invited them to forge the history of the Covenant. Israel's response to this invitation helps us understand and value the relationship between faith and history.

When God calls us to construct history, we are shown the road and the goal; God demands free and believing collaboration from people, and supports them in the challenges they encounter along the way. But it is not enough to know the goal and to walk toward it. We must also stop along the way, be sure we are on the proper route, and strengthen ourselves for the journey. On our way to the Father, we must discern the signs of God's providence in order to discover God's desire for our life.

This demands that we, who form the people of God, educate ourselves so that we will be capable of forging history. The United States needs young people who will act in Covenant with God—women and men of willing heart, capable of making the way of Jesus their own. The attitude of the disciple must be one of total trust, full coresponsibility, and faithful commitment, knowing that everything is in God's hands but also acknowledging that God acts through people.

Faith always implies a calling from God and our response to it. This calling is at the same time a gift from God and a task: a gift because every time we receive a calling from God and respond to it, our faith is strengthened, our love is intensified, and our hope is nourished; a task because we have to act firmly and work diligently to fulfill our mission. God's call always requires movement, conversion, change, and growth.

We strengthen ourselves as a people of faith. When the tribes of Israel fled Egypt under God's guidance, they made a Covenant with God and constituted themselves as one people. In the same way, the multiple ethnic and cultural groups of the United States should form a new people of faith. This is not easy, for although we have many similarities, we also have significant differences. We frequently fall into the temptation to turn against one another and allow our nationalistic hypersensitivities to set up barriers and lead to destructive competition.

To escape any kind of slavery, God demands effort and conversion so that we can transcend our limitations and be strengthened as a people. Love, the commandment of the New Covenant, applied to the various peoples of this country, is the guide for living in harmony and making the Gospel of Jesus a reality among us.

Jesus loved without limits and shared in the pilgrim life of every human being, both as a traveling companion and in the search to know God's will. He traveled constantly, without a fixed place of residence, coming and going to fulfill his mission. His goal was clear—to proclaim the arrival of the Reign of God. But how he proclaimed it varied according to the needs of his listeners and to how he discerned the best way to communicate his message to different people.

Jesus' attention to the signs of Providence made him see God's will for him to carry the Good News beyond the people of Israel. This led him to speak with the Samaritan woman and with the Syrophoenician woman, thus crossing the rigid boundary between his own people and other peoples. In this way he sowed the seeds of the Reign of God in all humanity. Being coprotagonists of history with God for us means following Jesus' praxis—carrying the Good News to all persons, with an emphasis on Hispanic people—but it also means being willing to hear God's call to carry the message of salvation to people of other ethnic and cultural groups.

Reflection

1. Form three groups, each of which will record its reflections on newsprint.
- The first group identifies three ways that young Latinos are coprotagonists with God in the history of the United States, contributing values that are characteristic of Hispanic people.
- The second group identifies three challenges presented by the society and dominant culture of the United States to Latino *jóvenes,* in their role as coprotagonists of history.
- The third group identifies three ways *jóvenes* can, without losing their own cultural identity, begin working with persons from other cultures and ethnic groups to form a single people of faith.

2. Each group shares its conclusions with the whole community.

Called to live the Gospel

Analyze the results of the previous reflection and discuss the following questions:

- To what is God calling you as a community of young Latino Catholics?
- What do you need to do to respond to this call?

Commentary 3:
Faith, hope, and love as driving forces of history

We have many ways of collaborating with God in the construction of history. Outstanding among them is daily life: how we live the routine events that come as a part of every person's life. Thus students contribute by studying, workers by working, parents by educating and attending to the needs of their children, adult offspring by caring for elderly parents, and so on within all the roles we fulfill during our life.

We also construct history by fulfilling our civic responsibilities and through our participation in personal and community development projects and social service. Artistic and cultural activities, such as dance, music, and painting, or passing on the traditions of a people, are other ways of contributing to the building of history.

All these activities and many others are performed daily by millions of people throughout the world. What makes Christians coprotagonists with God is the spirit with which they carry out these actions.

Young people often question the authenticity of the faith of older adults. Often young people's disillusionment with the church, religion, or Christianity is rooted in a lack of true witness by Christians around them. But it is not enough to question others in this way, we must also question ourselves.

People in the younger generation are called to be prophets of hope for other young people, and this implies truly believing the Good News, announcing it, living out what they believe, proclaiming what they live, communicating their faith experience, and, finally, bearing witness with their whole life that they are coprotagonists with God in history. In this way, youth and young adults build the road as they walk and as they invite other young people to participate in this great mission.

We make history through our experiences. To make history we must internalize the knowledge we acquire and the events that occur in our life. It is not enough to learn things or to know about what is happening in the world. We have to make these things our own and embrace them as experiences integral to our life, so that they become sources of motivation for action within our own social reality. Experience arises from life itself, and then returns to life again, this time transforming it. Thus comes the importance of living history consciously, making it our own, avoiding a life in which the days pass over us without our leaving any mark on the flow of history.

To construct history side by side with God, we have to live out our daily life, and all the projects and actions we undertake, animated by the spirit of God. Otherwise we make history in isolation, running the risk of leading history in a direction unrelated to God's loving designs for humanity. The forces that move history in keeping with the desires of God's heart are faith, hope, and love—the three fundamental virtues of those who follow Jesus.

Faith. Faith enables us to see humans and history as Jesus sees them—as originating in the creative love of God and with a destiny to live in eternal and loving communion with God. Through faith we know that life is a gift of the Father who loves and cares for all persons, individually and personally. Faith helps us to perceive God's salvation in every human event, to give to life its true significance, and to find the meaning of our own existence.

Hope. Hope is Christ's energy within us. It allows us to live the **first fruits** of eternal life in our present life. Hope is the power that generates a future in which every day we live fully in Jesus Christ; it is the source of a peace that knows that every good thing we do sows the fruits of eternal life; it is the source of the happiness that is born when we realize that good is more powerful than evil because it carries the power of the risen Jesus.

Love. Love is the result of faith and hope. When we see humans and history as God sees them, born within us is a desire to love them. From this love is born the yearning and the demand to be coprotagonists with God in history. That is, we want to give ourselves over to others, as God did through Jesus, in order to make fruitful the seeds of goodness that God has placed within us and within all humans so that we can live in love and solidarity.

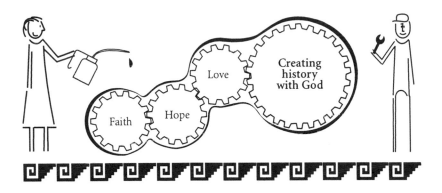

To build history with God, we need to open ourselves to God's grace and ask God to fill us with faith, bless us with hope, and strengthen us with love. The more we develop these three vital powers in our life, the more energy we will have to build history with God.

Reflection

1. Form groups of four persons each.
- Share with one another which of the three virtues—faith, hope, or love—most frequently finds expression in concrete acts in your own life. Give some examples.
- Share with one another which of the three virtues is most difficult to express in your life, explaining why you think this is so.

2. Ask one participant from each small group to share with the whole community what most impressed her or him in the small-group reflection.

Called to live the Gospel

Identify some concrete ways the community can help reinforce the faith, hope, and love needed to build history with God.

Celebration of our faith: Building history with God

Preparation. Bring objects that symbolize the building of history, making sure to have at least one for each person. For example, maps, hammers, Bibles, books, cooking utensils, or anything that is used to give direction to life, and therefore, to history.

1. Make an altar and place the symbolic objects on it. Play some background music, and give the following introduction:

> The objective of this prayer is to commit ourselves to participating in the struggle of our people for better life conditions, collaborating in this way toward the building of history. We have some objects that represent some important actions in history. Imagine the future we have in our hands. What a wealth of experiences, struggles, efforts, hopes, and fruits would be represented here if we all continue to be coprotagonists of history with God!

2. Take a few minutes to hear what God has to say to each of you in light of the message of this meeting. Write a few phrases in your book or diary that will help you to remember God's message.

3. Have each person walk to the altar and choose a symbol that motivates him or her to be a builder of history.

4. Form pairs, and give each other the symbol you have chosen, explaining to your partner why you chose that particular object. When your receive your partner's symbol, share with her or him some words of encouragement. Then say a prayer for her or him.

5. Sing a song about building history with God.

Christian Spirituality and Prayer

"Again, truly I tell you, if two of you agree on earth about anything you ask, it will be done for you by my Father in heaven. For where two or three are gathered in my name, I am there among them."

—Matthew 18:19–20

Overview

Objectives

- To see and appreciate prayer as a conversation with God
- To appreciate silence and the feelings of safety and security in our conversation with God

Plan for the meeting

Conversation exercise

Prayer of reconciliation

Illumination for a Christian spirituality
Commentary 1: Conversation between people
Commentary 2: Conversing with God

Celebration of our faith: The conversational word of God

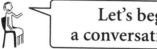

Let's begin with a conversation exercise

In this session we will begin with an exercise. Afterward we will pray.

1. Pair up and have one person begin by asking the first question. Discuss that question for two minutes. Then repeat the same step with the second question.
• If you could change anything at all in the world, what would it be?
• What would you like your grandchildren to tell their children (your great-grandchildren) about you?

2. Take a moment to reflect silently, and then answer the following questions in writing:
• What feelings or reactions did these questions bring up for you?
• What was your partner's reaction to the questions?
• What did you learn about the interests and values of your partner through her or his responses?
• What did you learn about yourself?

3. Form groups of six, composed of three of the pairs formed earlier. Share what you learned from the short conversations and the writing exercise, especially the importance of asking questions related to your values and to your expectations about the world and yourselves.

Prayer of reconciliation

Introduction. We will begin praying with our bodies like we did at the end of the fourth community meeting, "Celebration of our faith," on pages 75–77.

1. The person facilitating the prayer makes the following introduction:

> By practicing corporeal prayer, we get used to praying with our body, and we allow this type of prayer to become more spontaneous and habitual for us. In various cultures, corporeal prayer is common, be it through ritual gestures similar to those used in our eucharistic celebrations or through dances accompanied by music. As *jóvenes* in the United States, we can discover different ways of praying with our body to help us express our feelings toward God.

2. Invite the community to form a circle and enter into a spirit of reflection. Then lead the corporeal prayer three times.

3. Begin the prayer by saying the following:

> Father, all-powerful and ever-living God,

Everyone then joins in and reads aloud the rest of the prayer:

> we praise and thank you through Jesus Christ our Lord
> for your presence and action in the world.
>
> In the midst of conflict and division,
> we know it is you
> who turns our minds to thoughts of peace.
> Your Spirit changes our heart:
> enemies begin to speak to one another,
> those who were estranged join hands in friendship,
> and nations seek the way of peace together.
>
> Your Spirit is at work
> when understanding puts an end to strife,
> when hatred is quenched by mercy,
> and vengeance gives way to forgiveness.

For this we should never cease
to thank and praise you. . . .[3]

In Jesus Christ our Lord. Amen.

Illumination for a Christian spirituality

The exercise and prayer that we have just concluded placed us in a
spirit of conversation with God. The next commentary will help us
to delve into the importance of human conversation and enable us to
view conversation with God as a form of prayer.

Commentary 1: Conversation between people

Conversation is a source of enrichment that allows a leisurely exchange of views. Conversation entails persons learning from one another, sharing joys and griefs, or persons pouring out their heart.
Conversation sometimes is centered on making plans together, asking someone for advice, reconciling, or dialoging about a topic of
mutual interest.

Conversation is a form of communication that touches our
emotions as well as our mind. A good conversation gives us a sense
of being nurtured, spiritually healed, encouraged, or affirmed. Most
great saints, writers, and other artists have had friends to converse
with—persons who stimulated their creativity, persons who accepted who they were (even if they shared different views), persons who
they knew they could trust and talk to in times of hardship.

The quality and frequency of conversation affects many important aspects of our life. Open communication and enriching conversation lead to good relationships, strong marriages, healthy families,
and productive working environments. In contrast, when a person
lectures another person and mutual listening is absent, there is no
conversational spirit. When one of the parties becomes silly, stiff,
overly formal, or defensive, it becomes hard to converse, and the hu-
manizing benefits of conversation are lost.

To enter into a good conversation, it is necessary to feel safe and
secure, and this environment is created through trust and mutual efforts at understanding. If one party feels threatened, she or he will
clam up. The habit of seeking first to understand *before* seeking to be

understood is a key prerequisite to a good conversation. In such a setting, we can express not only our ideas but also our feelings. We can
reveal our true selves, offer and accept criticism, work through differences, and achieve that level of intimacy for which we yearn. This
experience of being accepted and affirmed enables us to do the same
for other people.

Reflection in community

- Share what you experience when you have a good conversation,
  and identify the positive results that ensue from it. On newsprint
  write out some of these benefits.
- Share the types of feelings and the negative effects that are generated when you have the need to talk to someone but for some reason cannot or do not do so. Write on the newsprint what negative
  effects result from not being able to converse about something important.
- Remember some occasions when your small community has had
  good conversations, and share your recollections.
- Identify two or three ways you can create a safe environment for
  having good conversations in your small community.

Commentary 2: Conversing with God

Conversational prayer is the simple act of talking to God in a familiar way, telling God of our concerns, asking for a favor or advice,
complaining, thanking God for blessings given, and telling God how
we feel. It is a conversation between friends, between two people who
love each other, between a child and a parent who is trusted and

loved. Such conversational prayer is easy and intimate, but it requires knowing how to converse.

How do we converse with God in the way that we converse with a good friend? Who can create the security necessary to converse with God, when it has been said that to see God's face is to die? What if we speak to God and receive no reply? How does one carry on a one-sided conversation?

We are not the ones responsible for creating an atmosphere of trust. It is up to God to create the trust and security needed for conversing with us. How does God do it? Let us take a look at one of the images that Jesus—who says that when we see him, we see the Father—used to describe himself by reading John 10:11–15.

Jesus teaches his followers to address God as *Abba*, a familiar word in Hebrew used to address one's father. It is the equivalent of "papa" or "daddy" said with the security and intimacy of a child.

Read Mark 14:36.

Jesus paints an image of himself, and thus of God, as one who cares in a special way about the hungry, the homeless, the naked, the sick, and the imprisoned. God cares about the least of the children and demands that those children who are healthy, well fed, well housed, and free share those blessings with those who for whatever reasons do not enjoy these benefits. Again the image is that of a compassionate God.

Read Matthew 25:31–46.

The Gospel of Matthew puts these words in God's mouth: "'This is my Son, the Beloved; with him I am well pleased'" (17:5). Our God is one who finds great delight in the human Jesus, which is

a sign that God too finds great joy in each and every one of us—creatures made in God's image.

Through the imagery of the Scriptures, God creates the feelings of safety we need to converse with God, and God responds to what we share. There we learn that our God is with us in order to save us, not condemn us; to gather us together, not scatter us; to heal us, not wound us. There we hear God's response of understanding and love, forgiveness and peace, motivation and affirmation, advice and correction, calling and mission, trust and encouragement.

What is our image of God? Is it the God of Jesus, or is it a God fashioned by faulty theology?

Personal reflection

- Identify some ways or occasions where you have had a good conversation with God. What factors, either external or internal, helped to facilitate your conversation? What was the conversation about? What were the benefits of this dialog?
- Identify some of the most common obstacles you encounter when establishing a conversation with God. Where are these obstacles rooted? How can you avoid or remove them? Do you need help to overcome them? Who can give you this help? Could it be your community or one of its members?

Reflection in community

Anyone who wishes to share her or his personal reflection with the whole community may do so at this time. Some people may prefer to share their thoughts and feelings with one or two of their peers. Keep ten minutes free for those who wish to share in private.

Celebration of our faith:
The conversational word of God

Preparation. Bring two 2-yard lengths of ribbon approximately 2 inches wide, one blue and the other red.

1. In the center of the room, place three chairs in a row so that each of the outside chairs is a yard from the middle one. On the outside chairs, two people will sit facing each other. Fold the ribbons in half and tie them to the chair in the middle so that each person in

an outside chair can hold in his or her hands an end of each colored ribbon.

2. Explain how to do the reading. Assign three readers: a narrator, a person to read Jesus' lines and hold the red strip, and another person to read the Samaritan woman's lines and hold the blue strip. While Jesus speaks, the person holding the red strip will lift it up. While the Samaritan woman speaks, the person holding the blue strip will lift it up.

3. Read chapter 4 of John.

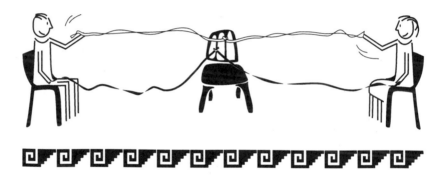

4. Offer a few minutes of silence, inviting the participants to pray with Jesus in the same way he prayed with the Samaritan woman. The following questions may be useful in initiating a prayer:
• If we found ourselves with the best, most understanding person in our town or city, what would we talk to her or him about? What would she or he answer?
• We know that Jesus is the best, most understanding person in our city. What do we want to speak to him about?
• Let us begin our dialog with Jesus, leaving enough time for some of the passages from the Gospel to resonate within us. In that resonance, feel Jesus' response to you, and continue the dialog with him.

5. Let us now reflect on the importance of silence in establishing a conversation with God. We need to gather our thoughts and

talk wisely to the One who gives us wisdom. Let us also thank God for the gift of hearing.

6. Pray this psalm in thanksgiving for the gift of hearing.

Facilitator:
Blessed are you, Lord our God, for the gift of hearing.

All:
In the fullness of our persons, we praise you, Lord our God,
    because you are a God of ten thousand gifts.

Facilitator:
We are grateful, in this prayer,
    for the marvel of hearing
    by which we can know the songs of creation,
    your unending melody of beauty,
    expressed in words, wind, and whispers.

All:
With open ears,
    we take in the joy of music,
    the delight of poetry
    and the simple songs of daily life.

Facilitator:
For all of these blessings, we are filled with gratitude.

All:
We rejoice that you have given us a third ear,
    the ear of the heart, an ear of the soul
    with which we may listen to silent sound,
    to the silent music of your divine heart.

Facilitator:
Help us, Lord,
    by quiet prayer and times of silence,
    to open that third ear
    and to heal the other two of all noise.

All:
We are also thankful
    for those persons who teach us how to listen:
    for poets, musicians,
    parents, prophets and teachers.

Facilitator:

Grateful are we, for that long line of holy people
   from the East and the West,
   who teach us to listen
   for the echo of your divine voice
   in all words of truth.

All:

For your powerful yet gentle word, Jesus,
   whose Good News cleanses our ears,
   we are especially thankful.[4]

Facilitator:

Help us now enter this time with a listening,
   attentive heart that we may
   be healed and strengthened by you.

All:

Blessed are you, Lord our God,
   for the gift of hearing.

Facilitator:

Lord our God, let our ears be attentive to your voice,
   and let our mouths speak the truth of our heart,
   that our conversations with you may be filled
   with grace and blessings.
   We ask this through Jesus the Lord.

All:

Amen.

Facilitator:

May the Lord bless us and keep us always in his love.

All:

Amen.

COMMUNITY MEETING

Evaluation of the Second Cycle of Community Meetings

A voice cries out:
"In the wilderness prepare the way of the LORD,
        make straight in the desert a highway for our God.
                                        —Isaiah 40:3

Overview

Objectives

- To evaluate the second cycle of community meetings
- To compare the evaluation of this cycle with the first evaluation to find out in which areas there has been growth and which areas require more effort
- To celebrate the culmination of the second cycle of community meetings with a prayer and a special gathering or outing

Plan for the meeting

Opening prayer

Conducting and analyzing the evaluation

Celebration of the culmination of the second cycle of community meetings

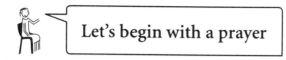

Let's begin with a prayer

The purpose of today's meeting is to evaluate the previous five community meetings. We will begin with a prayer on our experience during this cycle of community meetings.

1. Read aloud the epigraph for this meeting, letting its words touch your heart. Then silently answer the following questions:
• What deserts have you crossed since the formation workshop?
• What paths have opened, allowing God's presence to fill your life?

2. Ask the community members to form groups of three or four persons. Have them share their answers to the questions with their small-group members.

3. Invite those who wish to do so to pray aloud over some of the experiences that were just shared. All respond, "Hear our prayer."

Conducting and analyzing the evaluation

1. Conduct the written evaluation using form 4 in appendix 1, "Evaluation Forms," on pages 186–187. Ask each person to fill out all three sections of the form based on her or his own experiences. The community members will then be given an opportunity to share their opinions.

2. Discuss the written evaluation, based on the instructions given in the "Introduction: Community Meetings," pages 32–33.

3. Summarize the dialog about the evaluation, and record the most significant comments on the community's accomplishments and on the areas requiring more work.

4. Analyze the written evaluation by computing the average of each aspect that was evaluated and by making a list of the most significant contributions and recommendations.

5. Compare the evaluation of the second cycle with that of the first cycle by answering the following questions:
- In what aspects did we improve? What helped us to improve?
- Which aspects remained about the same? What can we do in the near future to improve these aspects?
- Did some aspects worsen? To what was this retrocession due?

6. Keep in mind the two evaluations and their comparison, and then decide what you need to do in order to progress in your journey as a community. Take note of these decisions, and file the evaluation and the conclusions of your reflection in the community files.

The evaluation also serves as notes on the history of the small community and its growth process. These notes foster a unique sense of identity in the community and may be useful for sharing the community's experiences with new members.

Celebration of the culmination of the second cycle of community meetings

Have a special gathering or outing.

Dialog with the God of Our Life

Then [Jesus] took a loaf of bread, and when he had given thanks, he broke it and gave it to [the Apostles], saying, "This is my body, which is given for you. Do this in remembrance of me." And he did the same with the cup after supper, saying, "This cup that is poured out for you is the new covenant in my blood."

—Luke 22:19–20

Overview

Objectives

- To remember the experiences of the initial journey, the community meetings, and the formation workshop in order to identify the word of God in our life
- To integrate the understanding that each participant has gained of his or her personal and communitarian Covenant with God
- To deepen the ways we can live out the Covenant through our relation to Jesus Christ

Program

Introduction. Welcome, registration, singing, refreshments, and orientation (1 hour)

Session 1: Meditation on our Covenant with God (2 hours)
A. Opening prayer
B. Overall vision of the Covenant
C. Creation of posters with personal symbols
D. Preparation of the meditation
E. Shared meditation

Session 2: Love, the Covenant, and personal development
(1 hour, 30 minutes)
A. A letter to a person you trust
B. Dialog in groups of four

Session 3: Created to construct history with God (2 hours, 30 minutes)
A. Reading circle to develop a creed and a commitment
B. Large-group session

Session 4: Our Covenant in Jesus Christ (30 minutes)

Session 5: The tent and the rainbow of the New Covenant (2 hours)

Session 6: Eucharistic liturgy and the rite of commitment (1 hour)

Session 7: Evaluation (45 minutes)

Preparation

The preparation for the retreat should begin a month and a half before the retreat is to take place (see the time line on pages 14–15). The retreat requires a team of facilitators who are responsible for the first four sessions of the retreat. Session 5 is the responsibility of the pep team. The liturgy team prepares session 6 and makes sure that a priest is contacted to conduct the eucharistic celebration. The evaluation team prepares the last session. A review of the section on the retreat in the introduction (page 12) and a review of the instructions for the initial journey (pages 17–18) may help in this preparation.

Session 1: Meditation on our Covenant with God

A. Opening prayer

To enter into the spirit of the day, begin with a period of prayer. Sit in a circle and invite each participant to say aloud a word that suggests the Covenant, such as *union, love, people, pact.* To conclude, share a prayer that asks God to strengthen, during this retreat, these aspects of the Covenant as we live them out with God and with our neighbors.

B. Overall vision of the Covenant

To help the participants gain an overview of the retreat, begin with an introduction to the principal dimensions of the Covenant. The *Catechism of the Catholic Church,* numbers 50–73, may serve as a basis for this introduction.

C. Creation of posters with personal symbols

A meditation contemplating five posters drawn by the participants will take place after the posters are finished. To make the posters, do the following:
• Form five groups; if the groups have more than twelve persons, divide them in half again. Assign one of the posters listed below to each group, and distribute the materials needed for creating it.
• Each person silently reflects on some significant ways she or he has lived out the Covenant with God in the dimension to be addressed in the group's poster. Then each participant chooses an important experience and represents that experience by drawing a draft of a symbol.
• Have the group members incorporate all the symbols of their group into a single poster. When all have finished, each person shares the meaning of his or her symbol with the small group, explaining how the Covenant has been lived in his or her life.

Assigning the posters

Group 1: The Creation. God created everything that exists out of love. Every created thing is good and is subject to the laws of transformation written into its own nature. Through creation, God communicates goodness and love. We human beings were created to receive and respond to this goodness and this love by orienting our life toward God and by ruling over creation for the good of all humanity and the glory of God.

Group 2: Grace. Through our baptism, God communicates with us and fills us with the divine presence, thus elevating us to the dignity of being sons and daughters. If before baptism we were already creatures made in God's image and likeness, in baptism God's grace enables us to share the life of the Trinity. Baptism gives us a new heart with which to love with God's love, new eyes with which to see life from the perspective of faith, and a new energy to use as co-protagonists of history.

Group 3: Freedom and sin. As human beings, our nature, like that of all God's creatures, is good. In contrast to other creatures, human beings enjoy the gift of freedom. This freedom allows us to live in Covenant with God or to say no to God.

Group 4: Redemption. God sent the Son into the world to re-establish communication with him and to seal the Covenant definitively, redeeming us from the slavery of sin and re-establishing the communion broken by humanity's misuse of freedom. When Jesus becomes the center of our life, we are new creations who share more fully God's goodness and love.

Group 5: History. We were created to construct history in ways that guide creation toward the end for which it was intended—to give glory to God. We glorify God when we extend the Reign of God in society, are good stewards of nature and its resources, and work for the benefit of all humanity.

D. Preparation of the meditation

Based on its poster's symbols, each group constructs a short meditation and a prayer to help the other participants remember this dimension of their Covenant with God. Each meditation should last about five minutes. The following example may help to prepare these meditations:

- *Title of the poster.* "The Creation"

- *Invitation to meditate.* We invite you to meditate on how to live out our Covenant with God in relation to *creation.* We have lived

out this Covenant with regard to creation in the following ways.
. . . Let us reflect in silence for a few minutes on why we live this
way.

• *Prayer.* We pray that the Holy Spirit will help us live out this aspect
of our Covenant with God more fully by . . .

E. Shared meditation

• Hang the posters in the style of the stations of the cross so that the
participants can walk in procession from one to the next.
• Choose a song related to the Covenant and practice it. The song
should have a refrain that can be repeated as the group walks from
one poster to the next.
• Have each group conduct its meditation in front of its poster.

Session 2: Love, the Covenant, and personal development

The facilitator makes a short introduction. He or she should explain
that the following reflection will be done silently, as everyone individually writes a letter to a person they trust, telling what they discovered as they remember their experience in the initial journey, the
community meetings, and the formation workshop. Invite the participants to go to a garden, the chapel, their rooms, or some other
chosen place with their book or diary to do this reflection.

A. A letter to a person you trust

Once you are in your chosen place, do the following:
• Enter into God's presence with a brief prayer.
• Slowly thumb through your book or diary, trying to remember
some experiences that helped you in your personal development.
When you come across an experience that has helped you develop,
make a brief note. Then choose the most meaningful experiences
to describe in your letter.
• Write to a relative, someone you trust, or anyone who has been significant in your faith journey. The letter should be one to two
pages long.

B. Dialog in groups of four

After the letters are written, form groups of four. Invite each person to share something—a special experience, something learned in the reflection, a particularly vexing question, a thought for the future, and so on. The idea is to penetrate as deeply as possible the theme of love, Covenant, and personal development, based on personal experiences.

Session 3: Created to construct history with God

A. Reading circle to develop a creed and a commitment

This session will start with a reading circle. Form six groups, making sure that in each group are representatives from each of the five groups that prepared the meditations in session 1. If the resulting groups are too large, they may be divided, and two groups may have the same reading. Assign to each group one of the listed readings. Follow the process below.

1. Each group reads aloud the passage it is assigned (including the biblical message). Afterward it discusses the following questions:
- What is the primary message of this reading?
- In what way does the message of this reading change, ratify, complement, or deepen the way you see yourself, your life, and God?
- What changes does this passage invite us to make in our relationship with God, with ourselves, with other persons, and with the rest of creation?

2. Based on this reflection, the group develops in writing its understanding of how it can bring alive the message of the reading in its present life. On two different $4\frac{1}{2}$-by-11-inch sheets of paper, write a paragraph: the first in the form of a creed; the second in the form of a commitment.

To write the creed paragraph, begin the phrase with one of the key truths of the creed we pray during Mass, for example: "We believe in God our Father who . . . ; We believe in Jesus Christ . . . ; We believe in the church . . . ;" and so on. The participants should finish the phrases by including an experience about their relationship with God. For example: "We believe in God our Father who made us intelligent and who gave us the will to help young people stay away from drugs."

To create their commitments, the participants pledge to change a behavior or to take an action by openly declaring their vow. For example, they might say, "We commit to support one another by . . ."

Group 1: Called to a responsible stewardship

All human beings are privileged creatures to whom God gave **stewardship** over the rest of creation. This stewardship implies responsibility. The misunderstanding of stewardship and the misuse of our freedom lead us to degrade creation. For example, cultural progress has solved many problems and elevated our standards of living, yet at the same time, this progress has had a destructive effect on nature; it has created an abyss between the rich and the poor; and it has celebrated the domination and oppression of the weak by the powerful.

Read Psalm 8.

Group 2:
God is the creator of history, and we are cocreators with God

God is continually creating. Creation is an open system, with laws of evolution written in the essence of all the various creatures of the universe. The power of God is made manifest in a creation that has its own life and its own laws. Human beings are capable of providing new realities. Unlike animals, we can be conscious of this and guide our own life toward the end for which we were created—to live in Covenant with God, and to construct history with God so that justice and love rule. God has given us life, and asks us to use it to generate justice, unity, and liberation—that is, to construct history together with God.

Read Isaiah 58:7–9.

Group 3: The universe and history reveal God

All creation is an expression or communication of God. Our individual and communal history is the word of God and the way toward God. This history is at once both great and small. In its greatness, it speaks to us of the power of God; in its smallness, it reveals to us human limitations. Our greatness as human beings implies a task, and it is in fulfilling this task that we give glory to God. We are not the center of creation; the stars do not revolve around us, nor does the evolution of history end in us. Our responsibility is to be transparent enough to show God within us—to be God's sacrament, to be a sign that history is built by following our Creator's plan.

Read Genesis 1:26–31.

Group 4: We humanize the world through our work

Work—our daily tasks and our professional and civic activities—is the natural means by which we exercise our stewardship of creation. Work allows us to convert deserts into oases, to transform dehumanizing situations into settings that promote human development, to redistribute wealth equitably, and to use power for the common good. When we misuse our freedom, work becomes an avenue for arrogance and the oppression of others, for destructive competition and selfishness, for justifying inhuman situations and the degradation of the environment. This Covenant implies a responsibility to abandon our egoism and to use work as an instrument for living in communion with God, guiding history toward the participation of all persons in the Covenant.

Read Exodus 18:16–23.

Group 5: Sin and the Covenant, two facets of human nature

The people of Israel became aware first of the sin of the Egyptian oppressors and then of their own sin, for it is always easier to see another person's sin, especially if it affects us personally and unjustly. It is later in Exodus (in light of the prophets' message) when the Israelites begin to recognize their own sins: their reluctance to struggle for their own liberation, their desire for a comfortable life, and their breaking of the Sinai commitment to God. Consciousness of one's own sins, and of social sin, are key for living out the Covenant. We must recognize the reality that we are sinners and that God constantly calls us to reconcile and to re-establish our Covenant.

Read Deuteronomy 9:7.

Group 6: The Covenant is to be lived and celebrated

The Covenant with God is not something of the past but something to guide us presently. The people of Israel understood it that way and lived it out. Year after year they celebrated the Sinai Covenant in their daily life and through their liturgy. The steps that the people of Israel used to live and celebrate the Covenant can serve us today, if we update them, as points of reference for our own living out of the Covenant. These steps are as follows:

- To remember the history of the Old and New Covenant, and to retell it to successive generations
- To hear what God asks of the people who are to live out the Covenant: uphold the new law of love as proclaimed by Jesus
- To hear God's promises to the Chosen People, for the Covenant is fundamentally communal. The whole people must be faithful to God.
- To be prophets proclaiming the Good News, moving people to conversion, and fortifying hope for a new and better world
- To celebrate the sacraments, repentant of our failings, open to God's work in us, and committed to continually living the Covenant.

Read Jeremiah 31:31–34.

B. Large-group session

1. Each group comes forward and shares its creed and its commitment. A member of each group tapes the paper on which the creed and commitment are written on to the wall, forming two separate columns.

2. The whole group together analyzes and enriches the work done in the six small groups, using the following questions:
- What shared themes appear in these creeds and commitments?
- Is there anything important that you want to add?

3. Divide the community in half. Ask one group to work with the creeds and the other to work with the commitments. Both groups do the following:
- Read aloud the six creeds or commitments.
- Make a synthesis of the creeds or the commitments by eliminating repetitions and joining ideas.
- Choose two people to put the creed or commitment list into final form for use in the liturgy.

Session 4: Our Covenant in Jesus Christ

We suggest that this session be done through a presentation by two people. To prepare it, we recommend the following:
- Read, meditate, and pray over chapters 4 and 5 of *Evangelization of Hispanic Young People*.
- Reread the commentaries for community meeting 7 in this book, on pages 103–109.
- Review the notes made during this stage of formation in order to integrate the personal experience and the Gospel message.

  The following ideas may serve as a guide to explain key theological concepts:
  - One point of entry into the mystery of Christ and of the human person is to define the person and mission of Christ in light of his two fundamental relationships: Christ as the Son of God and Christ as the son of Mary.
  - Jesus Christ is both divine and human. He embodies two natures united in one person, the Son of God. His divine identity is explained by his eternal union with the Father and by his union

with the Holy Spirit. His human identity is manifested from the day of the Annunciation, when God becomes God-made-human, the son of Mary.

- Jesus, from all eternity, was the perfect image of the Father. He is as much God as the Father is. The Father has given all his life and power to the Son, who became incarnated so that he would be able to reflect God's love as a human being.
- Christ came to save us by incorporating us, through our baptism, into his Covenant of love with the Father, and by inviting us to live as sons and daughters of God, brothers and sisters to him and to one another, and lords of creation and history.
- Jesus came to bring about the Reign of the Father. With Jesus, God intervenes in history to reign as the Father in the midst of humanity, liberating us from oppression and death. Jesus, through his Resurrection, showed us that the all-powerful God, in whose hands our life rests, is a God of life who loves us infinitely.
- In the Covenant with God, we find peace and joy in our life as the first fruits of the eternal peace and joy we will find in God. To achieve this, we need to have the same attitude as Christ (Philippians 2:1–11) and to learn to live as children of God (1 John 3:1–2). For it is in Christ that we have access to the Father in one Spirit (Ephesians 2:18); by performing the same works that he did, we will likewise reach the Father (John 14:8–21).

Session 5:
The tent and the rainbow of the New Covenant

Preparation. Bring rolls of crepe paper or wide ribbon in each of the seven colors of the rainbow to set up "camping tents" (approximately 15 feet in diameter). You should be able to write with large markers on the paper or ribbon. Each tent grouping is made by fourteen people, seven of whom hold the colored strands of paper or ribbon (see illustration).

To sum up the retreat's message, the group will build several tents with the crepe paper or ribbons that represent the colors of the rainbow. The tent represents the Temple of the ark of the Covenant during the Exodus; the rainbow is the biblical symbol of the renewed Covenant. Both represent the women and men who try to live out

the various dimensions of the Covenant of love with God and with their neighbors. The dimensions of the Covenant that will be symbolized in the rainbow colors of the tent are the following:
- red—love, forgiveness, and compassion
- orange—mutual help and support
- yellow—preferential option for the poor
- green—personal and communal prayer
- blue—building history together with God
- indigo—collaborating with God's creative activity through our own work
- violet—commitment to the Reign of God

1. The facilitator explains how the exercise will be done.

2. The community then forms groups of fourteen persons with each group divided into seven pairs. Each pair is assigned one of the dimensions of the Covenant mentioned above, and given markers and a fifteen-foot strand of crepe paper or ribbon in the color of the

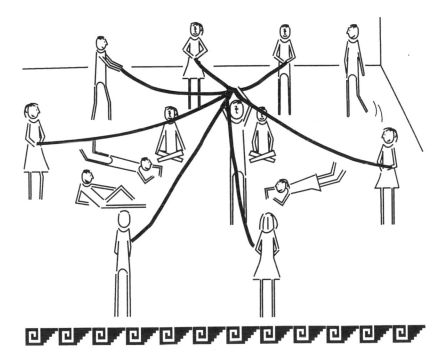

rainbow that corresponds to their assigned dimension of the Covenant. Then they write an example of how to live out the dimension of the Covenant assigned to them on the crepe paper or ribbon, leaving sufficient space at the end of the strip for a person to hold it when forming the tent. If any people are left over, teams of three people can be formed.

3. Each group forms its tent, following these directions:
• The tallest person in the group stands at the center of a circle formed by seven of the participants. He or she holds one end of all the strips above his or her head. This person symbolizes Christ, the source of the Covenant.
• Seven participants stand in a circle around the person who symbolizes Christ. Each one holds the far end of one of the strips, symbolizing the seven dimensions of how, as young people, they live out their Covenant with God and with others.
• Five participants sit or lie comfortably inside the tent, symbolizing the peace and joy of those who live out the Covenant.

4. After the tent is made the facilitator of the exercise helps the members of each tent to reflect, focusing on the following three key steps:
• One participant walks around her or his group's tent and reads aloud what is written on each strip. This person symbolizes the prophet who remembers the Covenant, emphasizes the duties toward the poor, promotes justice, and calls others to conversion.
• The facilitator invites the participants to reflect in silence, remembering the four central symbols represented in the rainbow tents— Christ, the dimensions of the Covenant, peace and joy, and the prophet.
• The colored crepe paper or ribbons are left lying on the floor, and all the participants sit down on the floor, forming a large circle. The facilitator invites those who wish to do so to express what they found meaningful in this exercise.

Session 6:
Eucharistic liturgy and the rite of commitment

The following is a guide to help organize the liturgy:

1. First reading: Colossians 1:15–20

2. Pray Psalm 104. The response is, "Send your Spirit to renew the face of the earth."

3. The alleluia is sung only if liturgically appropriate.

4. Gospel reading: Mark 6:30–44.

5. A shared homily is recommended, during which the participants reflect on the Gospel.

6. The offertory consists of the creeds, the commitments, and the strands of the rainbow.

7. In the rite of commitment, the participants form a circle around the altar. While background music is playing, the priest leads the renewal of baptismal vows. Afterward he turns to a participant, making a sign of the cross with holy water on his or her forehead, and saying: "The Lord invites you to continue living the Covenant with him. Enter passionately into the next phase of formation." The participant responds: "I will. I want to be a disciple of Jesus." This person then does the same with the next person, and so on, around the circle. If the group is large, two or three bowls of water can be drawn from the baptismal font, or the commitment rite can occur at several stations.

Session 7: Evaluation

The written evaluation can be done using form 5 in appendix 1, "Evaluation Forms," on pages 188–189. This form can be photocopied and duplicated. Give the participants twenty minutes to fill out the evaluation. Then facilitate a twenty-five-minute session in which the participants can share their responses.

How and Why the Bible Was Written

The word *bible* comes from the Greek *biblios,* meaning "books" or "writings." The Bible is a work of seventy-three books comprised of the Old and New Testaments. The Bible was born out of an apostolic tradition, which led the church to discern that the books presented the salvation story revealed to the people of God in an authentic and coherent way. This list of books, or **canon,** of the Scriptures was finalized in the third century C.E. Forty-six books make up the Old Testament (forty-five if the books of Jeremiah and Lamentations are considered one) and twenty-seven books make up the New Testament. These books were recognized as holy books and later as the sacred Scriptures; they are also recognized as the canonical books. From its founding until the present time, the church considers the Bible to be the word of God. As the *Dogmatic Constitution on Divine Revelation (Dei Verbum)* states, "For sacred Scripture is the word of God inasmuch as it is consigned to writing under the inspiration of the divine Spirit."[5]

The Old Testament

The authors and languages in the Old Testament

The writing of the Old Testament began around 1000 B.C.E. These writings document events in which the Israelite people discover God's presence. In general, they are written versions of an oral tradition passed on by the Israelites from generation to generation. A variety of people, united by their faith in a God who willed them to live as sisters and brothers, documented in those writings their experiences as the people of God.

Most of the Old Testament was written in Hebrew, which was spoken by the Israelites in Palestine before their Exile in Babylon. After the Exile, the Israelites began to speak the local Aramaic, but the Scriptures continued to be written and read in Hebrew. In Jesus' time the Israelite people spoke Aramaic in their homes, read the Scriptures in Hebrew, and used Greek for commerce and politics. Jesus attended school in Nazareth in order to learn Hebrew and understand the Scriptures.

The Israelites who emigrated from Palestine to Egypt spoke Greek. For this reason, in the third century B.C.E., a group of seventy-two Jewish wise men translated several books of the Bible into Greek. This translation, called the Septuagint, or the Book of the Seventy, included seven books—Tobit, Judith, Baruch, Ecclesiasticus, Wisdom of Solomon, 1 and 2 Maccabees—and some parts of the books of Daniel and Esther, which were not included in the Hebrew canon. These seven books are still included in the Catholic Bible, but not in the Protestant Bible, which adheres to the Hebrew canon.

The Old Testament reflects the history of the people of God

Much of the Old Testament was written during periods of crisis or transition, when the people of Israel needed to reflect more intensely on their experiences of the past in order to reaffirm their identity as the people of God and to seek out God's help for being faithful to the Covenant. As the people discerned God's design for them in their history, they became more conscious of being God's people, and they desired more urgently to pass on their history and to speak of what God meant in their life.

The principal goal of the Israelites when writing their traditions was to share their history of faith, not to describe historical events exactly as they took place. Reading the Scriptures in their communal meetings and celebrations, and studying them in the synagogues assured the Israelites that their faith would be transmitted to new generations, and allowed the faith gradually to grow and be purified.

As time passed, some writings came to be considered sacred because people began to realize that the writings helped them to discover God's presence in their life. In this way they gradually discovered that these writings were inspired by God, and they came to understand better God's intervention in their history: they attributed to God the Ten Commandments of the Law (Exodus 24:12); they asserted that God directed the written words of the prophets because their message came directly from God (Isaiah 30:8; Jeremiah 30:2–3); and they believed that their sacred books revealed God's authority, promises, and demands for faithfulness.

Later the Jewish people began to identify the books that expressed their faith more closely. These books were eventually placed on a list and used by the Jewish people to prescribe norms of conduct. The Jewish people made official the Hebrew canon after the Roman destruction of Jerusalem in the year 90 B.C.E.

The periods in which the Old Testament was written

1. The united kingdom of Jerusalem (1000–933 B.C.E.). The Israelites organize as a monarchy under King David, who is succeeded by his son Solomon. At that time, two hundred years after the events in Exodus, the legendary traditions about the patriarchs of Israel, and the reflections of the educated concerning the origin of the universe and of human beings are starting to be written. Some psalms and proverbs are also being written.

2. The divided kingdom: The Kingdom of Judah and the Kingdom of Israel (933–587 B.C.E.). The Kingdom of Jerusalem had been united for nearly seventy years. The economic exploitation during the reign of Solomon led the tribes established in the north to rebel and form the Kingdom of Israel. This kingdom, whose capital was Samaria, fell under the dominion of Assyria in 721 B.C.E. The Elohist tradition concerning the origins of the universe, the rise of human beings, the patriarchs, and the events of the Exodus were written during the time of this kingdom. The Books of Amos and Hosea were also written.

The Kingdom of Judah lasted from 933–587 B.C.E., when it fell into the hands of Babylon, and the Temple of Jerusalem was destroyed. At that time the Yahwist tradition becomes strengthened, and the two books of Samuel and of Kings are beginning to be written. Proverbs continue to be written. Micah, First Isaiah, Zephaniah, Nahum, Jeremiah, and Habakkuk are also being written at this time. The **Deuteronomic tradition** gave impetus to the reform carried out by a king named Josiah who brought to light laws that came from the north. These laws were completed and transformed into the Book of Deuteronomy.

3. The Exile in Babylon (587–538 B.C.E.). When the Kingdom of Judah fell, many Jews were deported to Babylon. There their faith was strengthened and purified, giving rise to Judaism, a new way of living the Jewish religion. This marks the beginning of the Priestly tradition. Zechariah, Ezekiel, Second Isaiah, and the Book of Lamentations are written during this period.

4. The Persian Empire (538–333 B.C.E.). Cyrus, King of Persia, takes over Babylon and allows the Jews to return to Judah. This is the time when the Temple of Jerusalem is rebuilt, the Priestly tradition is completed, and the first five books are organized into a unit. They contain the Torah (Law), which is imposed as the law of the state. The Chronicles, Ezra, and Nehemiah are completed. The works of wisdom are gathered, and the traditions that would produce Ruth, Jonah, Proverbs, and Job are starting to be put together. The Psalms are beginning to be compiled into collections that would soon make up a book. Second Isaiah is completed, and Third Isaiah is starting to be written.

5. The Greek Empire (333–63 B.C.E.). Alexander the Great expands the Greek Empire to Egypt, including Palestine. During this time, Zechariah and Third Isaiah are completed. Psalms and Proverbs continue to be written, and Malachi, Obadiah, Jonah, Job, Ecclesiastes, Sirach (Ecclesiasticus), Tobit, the Song of Solomon, Baruch, Wisdom, Esther, Judith, and First and Second Maccabees are also being written, as is the Book of Daniel. Daniel is written in an apocalyptic style that is characteristic of times of crisis. In addition, the Scriptures are translated into Greek.

The Pentateuch

The Pentateuch is the name given to the first five books of the Bible, which contain Mosaic Law. The authors of these books brought together various traditions. They sometimes wrote different versions of the same event, and at other times they mixed into one narrative events originating from different traditions. The following chart presents the process of integration of the different traditions that gave rise to the Pentateuch.

Outline of the Writing of the Pentateuch

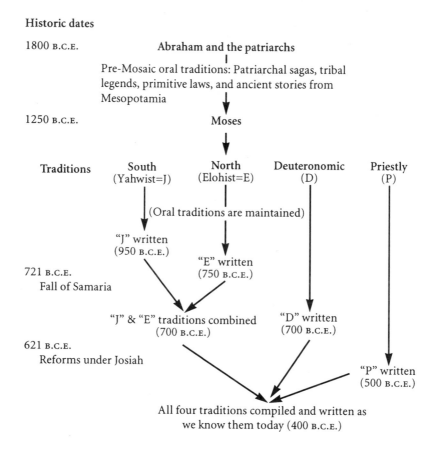

Historic dates

1800 B.C.E.   Abraham and the patriarchs

Pre-Mosaic oral traditions: Patriarchal sagas, tribal
legends, primitive laws, and ancient stories from
Mesopotamia

1250 B.C.E.   Moses

Traditions	South (Yahwist=J)	North (Elohist=E)	Deuteronomic (D)	Priestly (P)

(Oral traditions are maintained)

"J" written
(950 B.C.E.)

"E" written
(750 B.C.E.)

721 B.C.E.
Fall of Samaria

"J" & "E" traditions combined   "D" written
(700 B.C.E.)   (700 B.C.E.)

621 B.C.E.
Reforms under Josiah

"P" written
(500 B.C.E.)

All four traditions compiled and written as
we know them today (400 B.C.E.)

Divisions of the Old Testament

The Jewish people divide the Old Testament into three categories:
the Law (Pentateuch), the Prophets, and the Writings. They further
divide the Prophets into anterior prophets (Joshua, Judges, Ruth,
Samuel, and Kings) and posterior prophets (Isaiah, Jeremiah, Ezekiel,
and the twelve minor prophets). In the Catholic Bible, the Old Testament is divided into four parts—the Pentateuch, the historical
books, the wisdom and poetry books, and the prophetic books.

The New Testament

The New Testament* was written between the years 50 and 100 C.E. Portions of the New Testament were written in Syria, Asia Minor (Turkey), Greece, and Italy. Various cultures, religions, and socio-economic and political situations influenced how different writers perceived and transmitted the mystery of God.

In the first years of the life of the church, the disciples reflected on their experiences with Jesus, when he shared physical life with them and when he remained with them through his Spirit. The letters of the Apostles to the Christian communities were written first, then came the Gospels, followed by the Book of Revelation, or the Apocalypse.

The relationship between the Old and New Testaments

Both the Old and New Testaments were written to document the revelation of God, to keep alive the faith of the people, to guide and instruct the faithful according to God's plan, for solace and hope in the face of difficulties, and for guidance in straightening out the path when the people separated themselves from God's way. The *analogy of faith,* which consists of "the coherence of the truths of faith among themselves and within the whole plan of Revelation,"[6] must always be taken into consideration.

The Old Testament constantly refers to the revelation of God's will. Jesus showed his conviction regarding the authority of the Old Testament and used it as the foundation for his own teaching (see, for example, Matthew 5:18 and Luke 24:27–28). Jesus even attributed to God certain phrases from the Old Testament that the text itself did not claim to come directly from God (Matthew 15:4; 19:4).

The value of the Old Testament was affirmed repeatedly by the Apostles. Peter clearly said, "men and women moved by the Holy Spirit spoke from God" (2 Peter 1:21). Paul summarizes the way in which the early Christians saw the Bible when he writes, "All scripture is inspired by God and is useful for teaching, for reproof, for correction, and for training in righteousness, so that everyone who

---

*The second book in the Builders of Hope series, *Followers of Jesus,* has a document dedicated to the New Testament.

belongs to God may be proficient, equipped for every good work" (2 Timothy 3:16–17). In his Letter to the Romans, Paul says, "whatever was written in former days was written for our instruction, so that by steadfastness and by the encouragement of the scriptures we might have hope" (15:4).

Pedagogy of God and typology

From the Christian perspective, the principal objective of the history of salvation in the Old Covenant was to prepare for the coming of Christ. As a result, the books of the Old Testament reveal the pedagogy (education process) of the saving love of God.

Since the time of the Apostles, the Church has affirmed and explained the unity of the two Scriptures guided by typology. Typology consists of discovering in the actions of God in the Old Covenant, prefigurations of God's actions in the New Covenant through Jesus Christ.

Reading the Old Testament in light of the faith in Christ and having present the pedagogy of God and the typology helps one to discover abundant material in which to better understand the New Testament. On the other hand, the New Testament should be read in light of the Old Testament. An old saying helps to clarify the relationship between both Scriptures: "The New Testament is hidden in the Old Testament, while the Old Testament manifests itself in the New Testament."

The first Christians reinterpret the Old Testament

The paschal experience led the first Christians to reinterpret the Old Testament. They discovered that Jesus was the promised Messiah announced by the prophets and long awaited by the people of God, and that the entire universe is oriented toward Christ. They understood that the past was meaningful and valuable to the extent that it helped them to discover and live out God's new presence in Jesus Christ, Emmanuel, "which means, 'God is with us'" (Matthew 1:23).

With Jesus fell the veil that hid the deep and mysterious sense of the Law. Whoever reads the Bible from the Christian perspective and responds to God's call gives life to the letter of the Law, repeating salvation history today under the action of the Holy Spirit.

The writings of the New Testament hold the definitive truth of the divine revelation. Their main focus is on Christ, the incarnate Son of God, his works, his teachings, his Passion, and his glorification. This makes the Gospels the heart of the Scriptures, not only of the New Testament.

Biblical Literary Interpretation

The Bible was written over the course of many centuries, in languages unknown to us, and under sociocultural circumstances very different from our own. Each author wrote with a specific intention and used a specific literary form. When analyzing biblical texts, literary interpretive sciences are used.

Literary interpretive sciences for the Bible

The two sciences that concern themselves with analyzing, interpreting, and studying texts are **hermeneutics** and exegesis. Hermeneutics provides the rules needed to analyze any kind of literary text, with the goal of extracting its original meaning. It focuses on objective aspects of the text, such as the language, the historical epoch in which it was written, its literary genre, its immediate context, and the location of a passage within an overall text.

Exegesis is based on hermeneutics, but it goes further as it deals with the critical interpretation of a text. Biblical exegesis extracts the theological message contained in the text, analyzing the text under the light of faith, according to the Tradition and Magisterium of the church (see document 3, "The Bible and Our Catholic Tradition," pages 174–179). Among the noteworthy changes between ancient and modern biblical exegesis, the following two stand out:

1. The shift from exegesis with a dogmatic or moralizing focus toward exegesis with a theological approach. Exegesis with a moralizing focus tries to discover in the text the foundations of faith and Christian conduct according to what legal or moral authorities consider to be correct. A theological focus tries to identify the universal message of salvation that God offers through the text, and it also tries to discern a faith response to this message in ways that are relevant to the sociocultural and historical context in which the Christian community lives.

2. The shift from interpretation independent of the life circumstances of the Christian community toward an interpretation that brings God's message to life in today's circumstances. Interpretation independent of circumstances results in a series of rules that should be followed to the letter. Interpretation to bring God's message alive in modern circumstances tries to place the divine message in relationship to current problems, analyzing it and responding to it under the light of faith.

The exegesis carried out by the Magisterium of the church is universal, ensuring in this way a unity of faith among all Catholics and a deepening of understanding of the fundamental mysteries of the faith. But this universal interpretation needs to be actualized by members of the church according to their historical and sociocultural circumstances, so that all Catholics receive the message of the Gospel clearly and live out the central mysteries of the Christian faith. Actualizing the biblical message requires consideration of the following:

- the reality surrounding the Christians reading the Bible
- the key message communicated through the text
- the interpretation of the text within the church Tradition and the teachings of the Magisterium
- the call to conversion and to personal and communal action that God is making to us today through the word

Literary genres and symbols in the Old Testament

Many literary genres or styles exist, each one governed by different rules. Reading a history book is different from reading a novel, a poem, a play, a textbook, or a legal code. Each one awakens different expectations and attitudes. Failing to take the literary style of a text into account easily leads to confusion. Among the most common confusions that occur in reading the Bible are interpreting passages written to convey a religious message as if they were historical reports of a scientific character; reading exhortations and motivational statements as if they were laws; interpreting key teachings of Jesus as if they were unimportant messages; and viewing stories whose intention is to communicate a truth or offer a moral teaching as if they were literal histories.

For the past half-century, the Catholic church has taken special care to distinguish the various literary genres of the Bible. In his encyclical letter *Divino Afflante Spiritu* (1943), Pius XII says:

> When then such modes of expression are met with in the sacred text, which, being meant for [people], is couched in human language, justice demands that they be no more taxed with error than when they occur in the ordinary intercourse of daily life. By this knowledge and exact appreciation of the modes of speaking and writing in use among the ancients can be solved many difficulties, which are raised against the veracity and historical value of the Divine Scriptures, and no less efficaciously does his study contribute to a fuller and more luminous understanding of the mind of the Sacred Writer.[7]

Later, the Second Vatican Council (1962–1965) in its *Dogmatic Constitution on Divine Revelation (Dei Verbum),* clearly affirmed:

> The interpreter must investigate what meaning the sacred writer intended to express and actually expressed in particular circumstances as he used contemporary literary forms in accordance with the situation of his own time and culture. For the correct understanding of what the sacred author wanted to assert, due attention must be paid to the customary and characteristic styles of perceiving, speaking, and narrating which prevailed at the time of the sacred writer, and to the customs [people] normally followed at that period in their everyday dealings with one another.[8]

The following are brief descriptions of the literary forms in the Old Testament that usually need clarification:

Historical narrative. Historical narratives report events by situating them in the time and space in which they occurred, in order to tell what happened as objectively as possible. Examples include Judges, chapter 8, and First Maccabees.

Popular epic, or epopee. Popular **epics** recount historic events in a marvelous way that glorifies heroic figures and the actions of the people, in order to communicate an important didactic message. An example would be David's struggle with Goliath (1 Samuel 17:4–58).

The saga. A saga is a poetic, heroic, or mythological legend that converts events that occurred long ago, which were transmitted orally, into the historic experiences of a people; for example, the stories of the patriarchs (Genesis, chapters 12–50).

Didactic narrative. Didactic stories strive to impart a moral message or teaching. The Book of Jonah is an example.

The majority of the literary styles in the Bible use symbols and other forms of figurative language. Symbols are a way of expressing religious experience by fulfilling three functions: bringing us closer to the mystery of God, communicating the relationship between God and the community, and promoting the experience of God's presence in and among us. Symbols put the divine, the spiritual, and the transcendental in words that can be perceived by our human capacities. Some examples of symbols in the Old Testament are the following: the cloud, thunder, and fire to symbolize the presence of God with the people; the manna that symbolizes the nurturing support of God during the journey in the desert; and the rainbow that symbolizes the renewed Covenant.

We can summarize by saying that to perceive authentically the message that God wants to communicate to us through a text, we need to understand whether the human authors wanted to instruct or preach, counsel or accuse, pass down a law or witness to their faith. This is not to say that in order to read the Bible and pray with it, we must become experts in exegesis. But if we want to capture the truth that is contained in the Bible, we should, at least, take seriously the introductions and notes found in any good Catholic Bible.

The Bible and Our Catholic Tradition

In our daily life, we collect letters, stories, histories, anecdotes, and memories from the people we love and from events that have special meaning. All of these form part of our personal and family tradition, and this tradition gives a sense of meaning to our life. We also have a rich tradition of faith that begins with the revelation within history.

In order for us to know and appropriate both the familial tradition and especially our faith tradition, we must do so under the guidance of persons who are knowledgeable about these traditions. We know the Catholic Tradition of our Christian faith thanks to the Magisterium and to studies done by biblical scholars.

The efforts for approaching the Bible through biblical studies, the Magisterium, and the Tradition of the church are important but not sufficient. It is through reflection and prayer in community that dialog with the word of God becomes part of the concrete life of the church. In this connection of the word of God with the life of all faith communities lies the universality and value of the biblical texts.

Reading the Bible

The Bible can be read with a historic perspective, or it can be studied with a literary focus. However, to capture the word of God contained in the Scriptures, people need to approach the Bible with a faith perspective.

Christ gives meaning to the Bible

The Christian reading of the Bible, centered on Christ, gives meaning to the history of humanity. Christ's Resurrection finally revealed the goal of creation and the goal toward which history is directed.

When Paul provided a theological foundation for the decision to evangelize among the pagans, he affirmed "for in him all things in heaven and on earth were created . . . all things have been created through him and for him. He himself is before all things, and in him all things hold together" (Colossians 1:16–17). In his Letter to the Ephesians, Paul said, "'[Christ] came and proclaimed peace to you who were far off and peace to those who were near; for through him both of us have access in one Spirit to the Father'" (2:17–18). God's mysterious plan is "to gather up all things in [Christ], things in heaven and things on earth" (Ephesians 1:10). John synthesized this whole line of thought when he affirmed, "All things came into being through him, and without him not one thing came into being" (1:3).

The Holy Spirit helps us to understand God's revelation

Jesus had promised his disciples that he would send his Spirit to help them understand the truth (John 16:13). Only those who possess the gift of the Spirit can interpret spiritual things in a spiritual language (1 Corinthians 2:13); only they can understand what is "from God, so that we may understand the gifts bestowed on us by God" (1 Corinthians 2:12). Only the Spirit can remove from our heart the veil that keeps us from seeing in the past, the promised future (2 Corinthians 3:12–18).

God inspired the writing of the Bible so that God's wisdom would inspire our life. Paul, in his Letter to the Romans, expresses this in the following way: "For whatever was written in former days was written for our instruction, so that by the steadfastness and by the encouragement of the scriptures we might have hope" (15:4). Centuries later, in Vatican Council II, the *Dogmatic Constitution on the Divine Revelation (Dei Verbum)* states:

> Since everything asserted by the inspired authors or sacred writers must be held to be asserted by the Holy Spirit, it follows that the books of Scripture must be acknowledged as teaching firmly, faithfully, and without error that truth which God wanted put into the sacred writings for the sake of our salvation.[9]

Various ways of reading the Bible

When reading the Bible, it is important to recognize it as a dialog between God and the people. The Bible should, therefore, be read both in community and with a communitarian spirit. Through the Bible we can seek guidance regarding the paths we must choose in our daily life, but the Bible is not a series of easy recipes for every choice we make. To comprehend the history of salvation, we must approach the Bible as a source of new life and an experience of dialog with God in the following ways:

As a community of God within our history. God speaks continually to people within their history, from the moment of Creation to the end of time. This dialog does not begin or end with the written word. The Bible contains the sacred Scriptures of a people who recognized God's presence within their history of salvation. Today each community reads the Bible from within its own experiences, struggles, hopes, problems, and limitations; it is there that the word of God illuminates our life.

As a revelation of God-community. The trinitarian revelation of God (Father, Son, and Holy Spirit) shows us the option for a communal solidarity that is fulfilled in God's dialog and Covenant with all people. Even when we read the Bible and meditate on it individually, we can never separate it from its communitarian dimension. If we read it well, it will always lead us to the Trinity, refer us to the solidarity of God with his people, and call us to live in community. Catholics believe the word of God should always be understood in an ecclesial context because the text alone never fully captures the whole meaning of God's message. Thus we do not believe in the free and literal interpretation of the Bible by individuals.

As a continual offering of new life. Our dialog with God always generates life in us. Through this dialog, we find in the Scriptures many sources for a new life. Some of the most significant are the following:

- the awareness of our dignity as sons and daughters of God, created in God's image and likeness
- the acceptance of God's love and the grace to respond to this love
- the conviction of our salvation, knowing that God forgives our sins, liberates us from our oppressions, fortifies us in our pain, and gives meaning to our entire life
- the hope of achieving a full life through Jesus, the Christ, the Son of God who seals the New Covenant
- the action of God's spirit in the ecclesial community as a sign of the coming of God's Reign of peace, justice, and love
- the continual call to conversion and to bring the Gospel to those who need it and long for it

As a call to a mission. When we approach the word of God in a spirit of faith, we are able to listen to the calling to be witnesses to the resurrected Jesus. To bear witness to our faith is to follow Jesus' example. His attitude of prayer teaches us to seek God's will within our own historic situation. Jesus' response to the word of God motivates us to take concrete action to promote the Reign of God. Our participation in prayer, the sacraments, and liturgy complements our living out of this dialog between God and ourselves, the people of God.

The Bible, Tradition, and the Magisterium of the church

Catholics interpret the Bible under the guidance of the Magisterium and the Tradition of the church, which are assisted by the work of theologians and biblical scholars. The synergy of these perspectives assures us that we are approaching the truth God wanted revealed in the sacred Scriptures.

The Bible and Tradition

God wanted the salvation brought forth by the Son to be revealed to all peoples and to transcend time. Therefore, Christ sent his Apostles to preach to all nations the new life he came to bring forth to all humanity. To make sure his mandate could be fulfilled, Jesus sent his Spirit to the ecclesial community, who after Pentecost began to preach the Good News to all nations.

The Apostles and other disciples of Jesus' generation dedicated their lives to fulfilling the mandate through preaching and witness, the creation of institutions, and the celebration of their faith. In this way they began to transmit through word of mouth what they had learned from Jesus and from the action of the Holy Spirit.

This tradition, brought to life by the Apostles and carefully held by their successors through time, is known as the Tradition. The Tradition is different from the sacred Scriptures, although they are both intimately related. The sacred Scriptures are the books that hold the word of God and that were officially admitted as part of the biblical canon. The Tradition originates from God's word, is trusted to the Apostles and transmitted by the bishops, so that guided by the

Spirit of truth, they preserve it, present it, and disseminate it among all members of the church.

> It is not from sacred Scripture alone that the Church draws her certainty about everything which has been revealed. . . . Sacred tradition and sacred Scripture form one sacred deposit of the word of God, which is committed to the Church. Holding fast to this deposit, the entire holy people united with their shepherds remain always steadfast in the teaching of the apostles, in the common life, in the breaking of the bread, and in prayers, so that in holding to, practicing, and professing the heritage of the faith, there results on the part of the bishops and faithful a remarkable common effort.[10]

The Bible and the Magisterium

In the first stages of the church, the Magisterium (teachings) of the faith was generally recognized as a charism of the Holy Spirit given to a few faithful for the good of the community. There also existed a movement that assigned the Magisterium, in a special way, to the Apostles and their successors. Until the third century, the magisterial function continued to be seen in this way, and various laypeople like Justin, Origenes, and Pantemo were notable figures in the ecclesial Magisterium.

However, the apparition of the heresies and the multiplication of ordained ministries brought forth a greater control of teachings by laypeople, until eventually all the responsibility for doctrine was left in the hands of the bishops. The responsibility of safeguarding the full integrity of the teachings of the Catholic church through a pastoral leadership—the pope in union with the bishops—is known as the Magisterium of the church. In regard to the Magisterium of the church, the *Dogmatic Constitution on the Divine Revelation (Dei Verbum)* states:

> The task of authentically interpreting the word of God, whether written or handed on, has been entrusted exclusively to the living teaching office of the Church, whose authority is exercised in the name of Jesus Christ. This teaching office is not above the word of God, but serves it, teaching only what has been handed on, listening to it devoutly, guarding it scrupulously, and explaining it faithfully by divine commission and

with the help of the Holy Spirit; it draws from this one deposit of faith everything which it presents for belief as divinely revealed.

It is clear, therefore, that sacred tradition, sacred Scriptures, and the teaching authority of the Church, in accord with God's most wise design, are so linked and joined together that one cannot stand without the others, and that all together and each in its own way under the action of the one Holy Spirit contribute effectively to the salvation of souls.[11]

Evaluation Forms

Form 1: Evaluation of the initial journey

Evaluation of the sessions

1 = poor   2 = average   3 = good   4 = excellent

Session 1: Created to live in Covenant with God
Content   1   2   3   4   Process   1   2   3   4

Session 2: Lifelines
Content   1   2   3   4   Process   1   2   3   4

Session 3: Visualizing our future as adults
Content   1   2   3   4   Process   1   2   3   4

Session 4: Persons fully alive
Content   1   2   3   4   Process   1   2   3   4

Session 5: Liturgical celebration
Content   1   2   3   4   Process   1   2   3   4

General evaluation of the initial journey

• Coordination	1	2	3	4
• Hospitality	1	2	3	4
• Community spirit	1	2	3	4
• Advisers	1	2	3	4
• Use of time	1	2	3	4
• Site	1	2	3	4
• Meals	1	2	3	4

Contributions and recommendations

1. Which two sessions helped you the most? How?

2. What recommendations can you offer that may help in the planning and implementation of a similar event?

3. Additional comments:

Form 2:
Evaluation of the first cycle of community meetings

Evaluation of the meetings

1 = poor   2 = average   3 = good   4 = excellent

1. Created in the Image and Likeness of God
Content   1   2   3   4   Process   1   2   3   4

2. Our Dignity and Worth as Persons
Content   1   2   3   4   Process   1   2   3   4

3. We Grow in Community
Content   1   2   3   4   Process   1   2   3   4

4. Christian Spirituality and Our Image of God
Content   1   2   3   4   Process   1   2   3   4

Life of the community

	1	2	3	4
• Coresponsibility of all members	1	2	3	4
• Communitarian leadership style	1	2	3	4
• Evangelization and missionary efforts	1	2	3	4
• Prayer and spirituality as a community	1	2	3	4
• Commitment toward study	1	2	3	4
• Christian praxis of all members	1	2	3	4
• Community spirit outside of meetings	1	2	3	4
• Behavior as a community of communities	1	2	3	4
• Ministry of the *animador/a*	1	2	3	4
• Support of the advisers	1	2	3	4

Contributions and recommendations

1. Which meeting helped you the most? How?

2. Which aspects of your meetings need improvement? Give recommendations.

3. Which aspects of your community life have improved during this period?

4. Which aspects of your community life require more work? Give recommendations.

Form 3: Evaluation of the formation workshop

Evaluation of the sessions

1 = poor   2 = average   3 = good   4 = excellent

Session 1: God is revealed in history
Content   1   2   3   4   Process   1   2   3   4

Session 2: How to find books and passages in the Bible
Content   1   2   3   4   Process   1   2   3   4

Session 3: How to identify literary styles in biblical texts
Content   1   2   3   4   Process   1   2   3   4

Session 4: God's progressive revelation
Content   1   2   3   4   Process   1   2   3   4

Session 5: The Bible, Tradition, and the Magisterium
Content   1   2   3   4   Process   1   2   3   4

Session 6: Liturgy of the word
Content   1   2   3   4   Process   1   2   3   4

General evaluation of the formation workshop

- Coordination   1   2   3   4
- Hospitality   1   2   3   4
- Community spirit   1   2   3   4
- Advisers   1   2   3   4
- Use of time   1   2   3   4
- Site   1   2   3   4
- Meals   1   2   3   4

Contributions and recommendations

1. Which two sessions helped you the most? How?

2. What recommendations can you offer that may help in the planning and implementation of a similar event?

3. Additional comments:

Form 4: Evaluation of the second cycle of community meetings

Evaluation of the meetings

1 = poor   2 = average   3 = good   4 = excellent

6. A Calling and a Way
Content 1 2 3 4   Process 1 2 3 4

7. Exodus, Liberation, and Covenant
Content 1 2 3 4   Process 1 2 3 4

8. Jesus, the New and Eternal Covenant
Content 1 2 3 4   Process 1 2 3 4

9. Coprotagonists with God in History
Content 1 2 3 4   Process 1 2 3 4

10. Christian Spirituality and Prayer
Content 1 2 3 4   Process 1 2 3 4

Life of the community

- Coresponsibility of all members   1 2 3 4
- Communitarian leadership style   1 2 3 4
- Evangelization and missionary efforts   1 2 3 4
- Prayer and spirituality as a community   1 2 3 4
- Commitment toward study   1 2 3 4
- Christian praxis of all members   1 2 3 4
- Community spirit outside of meetings   1 2 3 4
- Behavior as a community of communities   1 2 3 4
- Ministry of the *animador/a*   1 2 3 4
- Support of the advisers   1 2 3 4

Contributions and recommendations

1. Which meeting helped you the most? How?

2. Which aspects of your meetings need improvement? Give recommendations.

3. Which aspects of your community life have improved during this period?

4. Which aspects of your community life require more work? Give recommendations.

5. Write down any suggestions you have to improve the meetings or the life of the community.

Form 5: Evaluation of the retreat

Evaluation of the sessions

1 = poor   2 = average   3 = good   4 = excellent

Session 1: Meditation on our Covenant with God
Content   1   2   3   4   Process   1   2   3   4

Session 2: Love, the Covenant, and personal development
Content   1   2   3   4   Process   1   2   3   4

Session 3: Created to construct history with God
Content   1   2   3   4   Process   1   2   3   4

Session 4: Our Covenant in Jesus Christ
Content   1   2   3   4   Process   1   2   3   4

Session 5: The tent and the rainbow of the New Covenant
Content   1   2   3   4   Process   1   2   3   4

Session 6: Eucharistic liturgy and the rite of commitment
Content   1   2   3   4   Process   1   2   3   4

General evaluation of the retreat

- Coordination   1   2   3   4
- Hospitality   1   2   3   4
- Community spirit   1   2   3   4
- Advisers   1   2   3   4
- Use of time   1   2   3   4
- Site   1   2   3   4
- Meals   1   2   3   4

Contributions and recommendations

1. Which two sessions helped you the most? How?

2. What recommendations can you offer that may help in the planning and implementation of a similar event?

3. Additional comments:

APPENDIX 2

Witnesses of Hope Collection

Series	Titles	Objectives	Phases of the Process
Prophets of Hope	Volume 1 *Hispanic Young People and the Church's Pastoral Response*	Analyzes the personal, social, cultural, and religious reality of Hispanic *jóvenes*, and the response of the church to their pastoral needs	Enablement of leaders and advisers
	Volume 2 *Evangelization of Hispanic Young People*	Focuses on the evangelization of Hispanic *jóvenes*, the model of evangelization used in small communities, and the role of Mary in evangelization	Enablement of leaders and advisers
	Volume 3 *Vision and Mission of Prophets of Hope: A Pastoral Process and Model*	Offers a process for experiencing the Prophets of Hope model and learning its pastoral-theological foundations	Initial experience of the Prophets of Hope model
Agents of Hope	Manual 1 *Dawn on the Horizon: Creating Small Communities*	Aids in the creation of small communities through a formation-in-action process lived and facilitated by people sixteen to twenty-four years of age	Creation and multiplication of small communities
	Manual 2 *Leaven in the Word: Growing in Community Life*	Helps the participants appreciate the meaning of community life and enables them to take responsibility for their own communities	Growing as a community for the well-being of society
	Manual 3 *Servants of the Reign of God: Advising Small Communities*	Helps train adults as leaders and advisers of small communities through an active formation process and pastoral practice	Enablement of leaders and advisers

Series	Titles	Objectives	Phases of the Process
Builders of Hope	Book 1 *In Covenant with God*	Fosters the vocation and mission of the members of the community in the history of salvation from a theological and anthropological perspective	
	Book 2 *Followers of Jesus*	Fosters the vocation and mission of the members of the community as disciples from a christological perspective	
	Book 3 *Acting Through History*	Fosters the vocation and mission of the members of the community in their immediate environments from a social perspective	Development of lay vocation and mission
	Book 4 *Committed as Church*	Fosters the vocation and mission of the members of the community from an ecclesial perspective	
	Book 5 *Fostering Culture and Society*	Fosters the vocation and mission of the members of the community from a socio-cultural perspective	

Animador/a, animadores. A person capable of sustaining the life of the community, promoting the discovery and development of the gifts held by members of the community, motivating each *joven* and the whole community, facilitating the prayer life of the community, encouraging hospitality and mutual support among community members, and supporting the community.

Anthropology, anthropological. From the Greek *anthropos,* meaning "man" or "human being" and *logos,* meaning "discourse" or "treaty." Science dedicated to the study of human beings in relation to their origin, geographic distribution, history, and culture; their race and physical characteristics; their socioeconomic environment, social relationships, and sacred practices and beliefs. From the theological perspective, anthropology reflects on the origin and nature of humanity and the reason that it was created by God.

Canon. From the Greek *kanon,* meaning "norm" or "rule." In relation to the sacred Scriptures, the canon is the official list of the books accepted by the church as part of the Bible. These books are considered to be inspired by God and as such to contain the norms for living one's faith and life.

Christian praxis. From the Greek *praxeo,* meaning "to do" or "to act." In religious language it is used to designate the interaction between theory (the analysis of reality, illumination with the Gospel, reflection, and evaluation) and the concrete actions of Christian people and communities. Christian praxis implies a process of personal conversion and the transformation of society.

Circumcision. A surgical operation to remove the foreskin of the male genital organ. For the ancient people of Israel, circumcision was a religious rite symbolizing their Covenant with God. It was performed by the eighth day after the birth of a boy. Initially it was demanded in order for him to be able to participate in Passover celebrations. Since the Exile it became a distinctive sign of belonging to the people of Israel and to Yahweh. Jesus was circumcised as dictated by law. Saint Paul broke with this tradition, liberating from it Christians who were converted from paganism. For Jewish people it is still a rite of initiation for entering into their community.

Communitarian. An adjective used to qualify the nature of an experience, spirituality, pastoral ministry, and so on, when it happens within the framework of a community.

Coordinator. Person who organizes and maintains the order of meetings and other community activities. The coordinator should delegate the role of leading different parts of a meeting or activity to various persons, who then take the role of facilitators. In the Prophets of Hope model, the functions of the coordinators and facilitators rotate among *all* the members of the small community. Coordinators also make sure that people responsible for specific services, such as hospitality and music, fulfill their duties. *See also* **facilitator.**

Coprotagonist. A person who shares in the principal action within a given setting. We define human beings as coprotagonists of human history because we collaborate with God in creating and giving direction to our history.

Deuteronomic tradition. The Deuteronomic tradition is based on a set of laws initially written in the Kingdom of the North. These laws served as the foundation for the religious reform carried out in Jerusalem by King Josiah in mid seventh century B.C.E. *See also* **Elohist tradition; Priestly tradition; Yawhist tradition.**

Economic neoliberalism. Economic and political system being developed in recent decades and highly influential since the fall of the communist system in Europe. It is based on a market economy and favors those countries, corporations, and persons who own high proportions of global or national wealth. It deepens the abyss between wealthy and poor countries and individuals.

Elohist tradition. The Elohist tradition originated in the Kingdom of Israel, also known as the Kingdom of the North. This tradition refers to God as Elohim. Its style is sober and monotonous, it has a more demanding moral code than the Yahwist tradition, and it is concerned with maintaining a distance between God and human beings. *See also* **Deuteronomic tradition; Priestly tradition; Yahwist tradition.**

Epic. The epic, also called the epopee, is a literary form that recounts historic events. An epic is typified by the glorification of heroes and an emphasis on supernatural intervention. Many stories from Exodus belong to this literary genre.

Exegesis. From the Greek *exegoumai,* meaning "to extract." Exegesis is a scientific discipline that analyzes a text, in this case a sacred text, to extract its original meaning with the goal of questioning the reader as to how to live or act. The exegete analyzes the text by situating it in its geographic, sociocultural, political, and religious context and by studying its literary genre and composition. *See also* **hermeneutics; literary genres.**

Facilitator. A person who leads a specific process in such a way that all the members of the community participate in it. The facilitator's principal tasks are to direct, or facilitate, an activity that allows all participants to have the chance to speak, to assure that the dialog remains focused on the designated theme, and to lead the community prayer. *See also* **coordinator.**

First fruits. This phrase means the beginning of something. In the context of Christian faith, the phrase is used to refer to the experience we have in earthly life of the fullness of eternal life with God, after our death and resurrection in Christ.

Hermeneutics. From the Greek *hermeneuein,* meaning "to express," "to interpret," "to translate." Hermeneutics is a scientific discipline focused on understanding ancient texts, especially biblical texts. Hermeneutics involves not only an exegetical analysis of the text but also the interpretation of the text based on a philosophical and theological perspective. Catholic hermeneutics analyzes the text under the light of faith, according to the Tradition and Magisterium of the church. *See also* **exegesis.**

Hispanic, Latino. In this book, as in the entire Witnesses of Hope collection, the terms *Latino* and *Hispanic* are used interchangeably to refer to people originating from Caribbean countries, Latin America, and Spain where the Spanish language and culture predominate, and their descendants who live in the United States, who may speak English or Spanish.

Jóvenes. The term *jóvenes,* plural of *joven,* refers to single young people, male or female, usually sixteen to twenty-six years old. *See also* **juventud.**

Juventud. The term *juventud* refers to the sociological group formed by *jóvenes. See also* **jóvenes.**

Latino, Hispanic. *See* **Hispanic, Latino.**

Literary genres. Forms of written expression such as historical narratives, poetry, drama, letters, songs, fables, parables, sayings, and novels. The Bible contains some literary genres unique to the epochs in which it was written. For more information on this topic, see document 2, "Biblical Literary Interpretation," on pages 170–173. *See also* **exegesis; hermeneutics.**

Prefigure. A person or event of the Old Testament is said to prefigure a person or event of the New Testament when they present similar qualities or characteristics. Abraham prefigures the promised Messiah because he is chosen by God; with him began God's promises to form the Chosen People, to bless all nations, and to take possession of the Promised Land. These promises are fulfilled in Jesus, God's Chosen One, who formed the people of God, made salvation universal, and implanted the Reign of God on earth.

Priestly tradition. The Priestly tradition started during the Exile in Babylon the years 587 and 538 B.C.E. It was originated when the priests reread their traditions and applied them to the Exile situation in order to maintain the faith and hope of the people of Israel. *See also* **Deuteronomic tradition; Elhoist tradition; Yawhist tradition.**

Sacrament. Sign and instrument of God's sanctifying action in people and in the ecclesial community. Christ is the sacrament of the Father because he is a sign of God in the history of humanity and an instrument of God's love, liberation, justice, and mercifulness. The church is a sacrament of Christ because it is a sign of the Risen Jesus and an instrument that makes the Reign of God present in the world. In the church there are seven sacraments or liturgical celebrations that are signs and instruments of the Holy Spirit's sanctifying action in various dimensions and moments of Christian life.

Stewardship. Stewardship is the careful and responsible management of something entrusted to one's care. In the Witnesses of Hope collection, stewardship refers to the role given to human beings by God in relation to creation. This translates into living a relationship of kinship with nature and the whole universe; developing a spirituality that celebrates the sacredness of all God's creation; taking care and administrating with justice our own personal material resources and those of the church and society; using the earth's resources, the culture, the sciences, and technology to promote human development while respecting ecology. The equivalent term used in Spanish is *señorío*.

Theology, theological. From the Greek *theos*, meaning "God" and *logos*, meaning "discourse" or "treaty." Study and reflection, and meditation that with the support of the Holy Spirit permits one to analyze the meaning of the revealed truth in an organized way. As a discipline, theology is the systematic study of God's revelation. In a broader sense, theology is a deeper understanding of the mysteries lived by the ecclesial community, achieved through a reflection on God's word taken as the basis of the community's historical experience.

Yahwist tradition. The Yahwist tradition originated in the Kingdom of Judah, also known as the Kingdom of the South. It presents a theological reflection on human nature and emphasizes the Covenant between God and God's people. In the Yahwist tradition God is referred to as Yahweh, as was revealed to Moses. *See also* **Deuteronomic tradition; Elohist tradition; Priestly tradition.**

1. Paul VI, *On the Development of Peoples (Populorum Progressio)* (Washington, DC: United States Catholic Conference [USCC], 1967), 7–8.

2. Paul VI, *A Call to Action: On the Occasion of the Eightieth Anniversary of the Encyclical "Rerum Novarum" (Octagesima Adveniens)* (Washington, DC: USCC, 1971), 10.

3. Bishops' Committee on the Liturgy, *Eucharistic Prayers for Masses with Children and for Masses of Reconciliation* (Washington, DC: National Conference of Catholic Bishops, 1975), 40.

4. Edward Hays, *Prayers for the Domestic Church* (Easton, KS: Forest of Peace Books, 1979), 55.

5. *Dogmatic Constitution on Divine Revelation (Dei Verbum)*, in *The Documents of Vatican II*, Walter M. Abbot, ed. (New York: America Press, 1966), no. 9.

6. Libreria Editrice Vaticana, *Catechism of the Catholic Church*, translated by the USCC (Washington, DC: USCC, 1994), no. 114.

7. Pius XII, *Divino Afflante Spiritu*, in *Rome and the Study of Scripture: A Collection of Papal Enactments* (Saint Meinrad, IN: Grail Publications, 1958), 99.

8. *Dei Verbum*, no. 12.

9. *Dei Verbum*, no. 11.

10. *Dei Verbum*, nos. 9 and 10.

11. *Dei Verbum*, no. 10.

Acknowledgments *(continued)*

The scriptural quotations in this book are from the New Revised Standard Version of the Bible. Copyright © 1989 by the Division of Christian Education of the National Council of the Churches of Christ in the United States of America. All rights reserved.

The psalms in this book are from *Psalms Anew: In Inclusive Language,* compiled by Nancy Schreck and Maureen Leach (Winona, MN: Saint Mary's Press, 1986). Copyright © 1986 by Saint Mary's Press. All rights reserved.

The quote on page 62 is by Pope Paul VI from *On the Development of Peoples (Populorum Progressio)* (Washington, DC: United States Catholic Conference [USCC], 1967), pages 7–8. Copyright © 1967 by the Libreria Editrice Vaticana, 00120 Città del Vaticano. Used with permission.

The quote on page 128 is by Pope Paul VI from *A Call to Action: On the Occasion of the Eightieth Anniversary of the Encyclical "Rerum Novarum" (Octagesima Adveniens)* (Washington, DC: USCC, 1971), page 10. Copyright © 1971 by the USCC. Used with permission of the Pontifical Council for Justice and Peace.

The quote on pages 137–138 is by the Bishops' Committee on the Liturgy, *Eucharistic Prayers for Masses with Children and for Masses of Reconciliation* (Washington DC: National Conference of Catholic Bishops [NCCB], 1975), page 40. Copyright © 1975 by the Bishops' Committee on the Liturgy, NCCB. English translation of *Eucharistic Prayers for Masses of Reconciliation* copyright © 1975 by the International Committee on English in the Liturgy. All rights reserved. Used with permission.

The quote on pages 143–144 is by Edward Hays, *Prayers for the Domestic Church* (Easton, KS: Forest of Peace Books, 1979), page 55. Copyright © 1979 by Forest of Peace Publishing, 251 Muncie Road, Leavenworth, KS 66048. Used with permission.

The quotes on page 162, 172, 175, 178, and 178 are from *Dogmatic Constitution on Divine Revelation (Dei Verbum),* in *The Documents of Vatican II,* ed. Walter M. Abbot (New York: America Press, 1966), nos. 9; 12; 11; 9 and 10; and 10, respectively. Copyright © 1966 by the America Press.

The quote on pages 167 is from the *Catechism of the Catholic Church,* by the Libreria Editrice Vaticana 00120 Città del Vaticano, translated by the USCC (Washington, DC: USCC, 1994), no. 114. English translation copyright © 1994 by the USCC—Libreria Editrice Vaticana. Used with permission.

The quote on page 172 is by Pope Pius XII, *Divino Afflante Spiritu,* in *Rome and the Study of Scripture: A Collection of Papal Enactments* (Saint Meinrad, IN: Grail Publications, 1958), page 99. Copyright © 1958 by Saint Meinrad's Abbey.